31 Words to Create an Organized Life

Simple Strategies and Expert Advice to Win the Battle against Chaos and Clutter

A Simple Guide to Create Habits that Last

MARCIA ZINA MAGER

INNER OCEAN PUBLISHING

Maui · San Francisco

Inner Ocean Publishing, Inc.
P.O. Box 1239
Makawao, Maui, HI 96768-1239
www.innerocean.com

Cover and book design by Yoori Kim

Inner Ocean Publishing is a member of Green Press Initiative, a nonprofit program dedicated to supporting publishers in their efforts to reduce their use of fiber sourced from endangered forests. We elected to print this title on 50% postconsumer recycled paper with the recycled portion processed chlorine free. As a result, we have saved the following resources: 1 tree, 944lbs of solid waste, 8,085 gallons of water, 2,250 lbs of net greenhouse gases, 17 million BTU's (Source: Environmental Defense Paper Calculator). For more information on the Green Press Initiative, visit http://www.greenpressinitiative.org.

PUBLISHER CATALOGING-IN-PUBLICATION DATA
    31 words to create an organized life : simple strategies and expert advice to
    win the battle against chaos and clutter/ Marcia Zina Mager. Maui :
Inner Ocean, 2006.
    p. ; cm.
    ISBN-13: 978-1-930722-60-6
    ISBN-10: 1-930722-60-5
    A month-long guide to help you prioritize, schedule, and simplify your life.
1. Orderliness. 2. Housekeeping. 3. Storage in the home. 4. Time management.
I. Mager, Marcia Zina, 1968- II. Thirty-one words to create an organized life.

TX309.T55 2006
648.8—dc22   0611

Printed in the United States of America
05 06 07 08 09 10 DATA 10 9 8 7 6 5 4 3 2 1

DISTRIBUTED BY PUBLISHER'S GROUP WEST
For information on promotions, bulk purchases, premiums, or educational use, please contact: 866.731.2216 or sales@innerocean.com.

Dedication

This book is dedicated to my husband, Dennis, and my son, Reyn.

From the bottom of my heart, thank you, for your never-ending love and support.

Acknowledgements

Mahalo nui loa (thank you very much) to Karen Bouris. I couldn't ask for a more generous or kindhearted publisher.

Heartfelt thanks to my editor, Angela Watrous, for her clarity, flexibility, and focus. And a round of applause to the rest of the dedicated folks at Inner Ocean whose hard work made this book happen.

And a special thank you to all the experts I interviewed who took time out from their busy lives to share their wisdom.

Introduction

Six months ago, I would have died before letting anyone peek inside my closets.

They were a nightmare. Half-gallon plastic bottles of stale drinking water (in case of hurricanes) shoved onto dusty shelves. Toys, puzzles, and games piled precariously on top of one another. Bottles of glitter and acrylic paint squeezed up against jars of paintbrushes, knitting needles, and skeins of wool, all of which I haven't touched in years. Baskets and hat boxes stuffed with colorful remnants, in case I ever decide to take up sewing. Coat hooks holding too many rain jackets and canvas shopping bags. Black patent leather tap shoes my friend Heidi gave me when she moved to Colorado, in hopes I would finally register for that dance class I've been talking about for years. Not to mention the loose vacuum cleaner parts and the sloppily folded wrapping paper and ribbons I was "recycling" from gifts I'd received in the past. Did I mention that this was just my downstairs hall closet?!

Then there were my appointment calendars...

I had three. One downstairs in the kitchen, another one hanging in my office, and the cheap day planner I carried around in my bag. Not that this system was working. I regularly forgot appointments, double booked myself, and ended up running around like a nut trying to fit in everything I had to do. And I swear, I'd been meaning to straighten up my desk and file for months. I was also having trouble finding important phone numbers in my overstuffed Rolodex (maybe because I filed people's names under a random system of first names, last names, or nick-names, depending on my mood).

I always vowed to clean up my act, but whenever I decided to begin and took one peek inside that hall closet (which wasn't easy, since simply opening the door involved having Scrabble and Candyland fall on my head), I'd blanch, slam the door shut, and find myself back to a very cluttered square one.

I was stressed and stuck, and my closets were living proof. Experts of feng shui, the ancient Chinese science of organizing space so that positive energy flows everywhere, believe that clutter and chaos in your closet, home, office, or life is a reflection of a muddled inner life. In other words, you can't get organized on the outside without taking a look at what goes on inside.

As embarrassing as it is to admit, I obviously needed this book myself. I started the research with a combination of excite-ment, interest, and a hearty dose of fear: What if I was incapable of getting organized? What if organization was "in the genes"? What if there were no real answers?

Slowly and tentatively, I began to try out the techniques and tips I was learning. Start small, all the experts told me, so I began with a junk drawer. Get help, they suggested, so I asked friends for support. Focus on what's important, they insisted, so I examined my goals and values. Buy less stuff, they empha-sized, so I started reducing and recycling. Gradually, things began to improve.

The good news for you in all of this is that this book was researched from the very messy front lines of my life; it was writ-ten from the untidy trenches of a disorganized battlefield. And the really good news is that not only did I survive, I'm thriving. The battle of the bulging closet is over. The scheduling catastrophes are no more. Victory is mine! Every expert tip and piece of advice I uncovered is actually doable and uncomplicated. My newly ordered hall closet and calendar are proof that these strategies work!

So take heart. Creating an organized life is entirely possible. Whether you want to manage your time so you can relax more, clean your home so you can feel nourished and at ease, or get your office in order so you can be productive and successful, the process of getting organized—inside and out—that's described in this book isn't difficult or stressful or overwhelming. It doesn't take years of study to understand. It takes applying just thirty-one simple ideas (which you can complete in thirty-one days if you choose). And by picking up this tidy little book, you've taken a very big and very orderly first step.

Focus

Getting Clearer on Who You Are and What You Really Want

"If you're not sure where you're going,
you'll probably end up somewhere else."
—ANONYMOUS

Before you throw away a single piece of clutter, you need to realize that getting organized is an inside job. It's a job that requires facing our inner clutter even before we face the piles of magazines and shelves of knickknacks. We need to understand why being organized is truly important to us and to the people around us, and how it can impact our everyday life. In order to do so, we have to get to know ourselves better. And that's what this section is all about—how to focus more clearly on who you are and what really matters to you. You'll get in touch with your life dreams, vividly imagine those dreams and desires coming true, acknowledge the uncomfortable feelings that rise up when you try to bring more order into your home, learn how to work with your unique personality, and discover what really motivates and pleases you—all of these are foundational steps that lay the groundwork for creating a more organized life.

Understand

Did you know that Americans waste millions of hours every day looking for misplaced or lost items such as keys, mail, eyeglasses, receipts, and other mundane stuff? And the average business executive wastes weeks every year searching for lost documents in messy files and desks?

When we're not searching for our stuff, we're buying it. According to the National Association of Professional Organizers (NAPO), we never even use 80 percent of the things we purchase! Yet cleaning experts suggest that if we simply reduced the amount of clutter surrounding us, a whopping 40 percent of our housework would be completely eliminated. And most of us feel overwhelmed from too little time and too much to do.

Okay, so we're messy, we're disorganized, and we mismanage time. In the grand scheme of things, does it really matter?

Absolutely, insist organizational and time management experts. The word "clutter" actually comes from the verb "to clot." Feng shui consultant Kathleen Thurston explains, "It's like having clogged arteries. The heart of the home gets choked. Our life intentions get obscured in a sea of random clutter."

And mismanaging our schedules is no different, adds organizational expert Don Aslett: "Wasting time means less quality time to spend with your family, your friends, and yourself."

In other words, clutter and disorganization—whether it's in our closet or on our calendar—rob us of the harmony and happiness we and our loved ones deserve. Clutter leaves us feeling tired, says Thurston, and keeps us stuck in the past, "creating mental patterns of procrastination, and feelings of overwhelm. It restricts and confuses our possibilities." Disorganization makes us feel busier and more pressured than we actually are.

"Time is life," points out time management expert Harold Taylor: "To get the most out of life, we must manage time well." Simply put, we're mortal. The time we spend with family and friends is not unlimited. Do we want to waste it because of bad habits, poor management, and disorganization?

The negative impact of being disorganized isn't limited to missed appointments or misplaced keys. Not knowing where to put things, not understanding how to plan our time, and not being able to meet our goals can contribute to depression, anxiety, anger, low self-esteem, failed careers, unhappy families, divorce, and even death. In fact, according to the Institute of Medicine, tens of thousands of people die every year, due in part to confused, mismanaged, and disorganized medical data and information.

But, hey, if death and illness don't inspire us to tackle those messy files, what about the cost in cold, hard cash? According to NAPO, more than one-fifth of us pay our bills late because we can't find the necessary paperwork, and 20 percent of our annual income is spent on "crisis purchases"— duplicates of papers, misplaced items, rush shipping costs, credit card finance charges, and impulsive shopping for things we don't actually need.

When we don't know how to manage our time and balance our lives, we become victims of a new social phenomenon called "job spill." Job spill means that instead of taking a racy novel to our timeshare in Maui, we take our cell phone and laptop. And since the majority of all our medical expenses are directly stress related, it's no surprise that job stress costs U.S. businesses billions of dollars annually.

So getting organized can make a tangible difference in the quality of our lives. It's liberating and empowering, reduces stress, and frees us to spend more time enjoying the people and things that are important to us.

But don't panic. I'm not saying you need to color code every pair of socks in your sock drawer or account for every second of your day. There are degrees of organization, and ultimately you get to decide how organized or spontaneous you want to be. This is about enhancing your life, not enslaving it. Give these simple techniques and strategies a try and then see how you feel afterwards. You might be delightfully surprised! And if you don't want this book to end up as another piece of clutter collecting dust in your bookcase, it's time to get started.

Think of a recent situation in your life in which being disorganized negatively impacted the quality of your life, your loved ones, or something else important to you. Then get a sheet of paper and write the following questions at the top: How would my life be improved if I became more organized? How would my relationships be enhanced if I managed my time better? What is my disorganization costing me in terms of time, money, appreciation from others, and self-respect? What's been holding me back from making the effort to change? Why is it important to me now to try something different? What will it take for me to commit to this process?

Write down your answers as honestly as possible. This is for you and only you. There's no need to judge or criticize yourself; just explore and see what you uncover. Understanding and self-awareness is the first step to change.

Clarify

Suzanne was fed up with her apartment and her life. For years, she'd been living with tattered used furniture and piles of stuff everywhere. Entering the living room made her feel awful. She was single, not by choice, and battling clutter and chaos everywhere. So one night, after a pity-me-party for one, she grabbed her journal and began writing furiously. Where did she really want to go with her life? What were her deepest dreams and desires? What kind of person did she want to be? What kind of life did she truly want to have? What was preventing her from creating it? Her writing unleashed a powerful burst of I'm-not-gonna-take-it-anymore energy, and she began to clean up her act. Piles of unopened mail, faded receipts, half-knitted sweaters, and unread books were sorted, tossed, or filed away. The Salvation Army happily carted off her mismatched furniture while a brand-new elegant couch and love seat found their way into her home. Slowly, her surroundings became more serene and welcoming. Then, one day when she least expected it, the man of her dreams knocked on her front door. (It was the UPS driver who was delivering her new closet organizing system.) No longer embarrassed about her home, she invited him in for a cup of coffee. And they've been snuggled happily on her new couch ever since.

The moral of this true story? There's a direct connection, as strange as it seems, between getting organized and getting what you want. "Set goals and start cleaning," insists consultant Michelle Passoff, author of *Lighten Up! Free Yourself from Clutter*, "What does organizing your closet have to do with living your dreams? Suspend your disbelief and see what happens."

Organizing "is a critical ingredient to success," says Passoff. And not the success of winning the Martha Stewart Neatnik Award–success in terms of gaining more fulfillment in your life.

Feng shui consultant Kathleen Thurston suggests that when it comes to organizing any area of your life, intention is key, "In the process of decluttering and organizing, the background for everything is our intention." But she's not just talking about our intention to have a perfectly ordered pantry. Instead, both Thurston and Passoff encourage us to clarify our broadest life intentions—to acknowledge everything we deeply desire in our hearts. You need to know what's meaningful to you before you decide where you want to be headed. These experts believe that if we clarify our life intentions and then begin what appears to be the unrelated, mundane task of reorganizing our bookcases and calendars, something extraordinary may occur.

How does clearing a path through your mess lead to your dreams? "There's a practical synchronicity," asserts Passoff. "If you're wanting a new job and begin cleaning the clutter off your desk and reorganizing your files, you may stumble across a business card of someone who ends up offering you a new career." So whether you believe there's magic operating here or not, "just suspend disbelief," says Passoff, "and you'll impact all areas of your life." Besides, she adds, "it's more fun to organize the way I say to than to do it so you can get the Good Housekeeping Seal of Approval."

EXERCISE

With a pad or journal, spend time writing about what you really want in your life. Look at all the major areas, such as personal growth, home, finances, time, relationships, career, health, and spirituality. First briefly describe your current situation in each area and clarify anything that doesn't feel good about it. For example, "I don't have enough time for traveling," "My house is so messy I don't feel like I can relax in it," or "I'm bored at my job." The clearer you are about what you don't want, the easier it will be to clarify what you do want. Then begin describing what you really want in each area, remembering to describe how you'd feel once you achieved these goals. Be as specific and detailed as you want. And don't be afraid to dream big.

To complement this process, create a Fulfillment Box using any kind of small jar or container. Write down on slips of paper the specific things you desire, such as finding your soul mate, losing weight, having more time to play, writing that novel, traveling to Italy, having orderly kitchen cabinets, enjoying a beautiful office, or having a greater sense of peacefulness in your home. Then drop each wish into the container. As you read this book and begin to organize your life, use the Fulfillment Box to enhance your progress. Whenever it feels right, pull out a slip of paper, say a prayer (or any words that inspire you) and burn the paper. You can even bury the ashes in the earth as a symbol of new growth. This can become an ongoing ritual that reminds you of your intentions and also gently inspires you to keep letting go.

Envision

Napoleon Hill, one of America's most famous motiva-
tional authors, said, "God has given us control over one
thing in our lives—our thoughts"

But what does that have to do with a messy closet?

Turns out, everything. What Hill really means is that
whatever we accomplish (or don't accomplish) in our lives
begins with our mind. All successful action, he says, always
begins first as a thought or idea. So in our quest to become
more organized, we must actually begin by envisioning.

Take Bertha, for example. She had just moved into a new
house and her home office was piled high with dozens of
unpacked boxes. Every time she looked at those boxes, she felt
completely overwhelmed. The task of unpacking them was
daunting. Day after day, she kept putting it off. Soon she
began feeling really bad about herself. Things rapidly spiraled
downhill from there.

One day, a wise friend suggested to Bertha that she imagine the room already organized. At first Bertha thought the

suggestion was ridiculous. But she respected her friend so she tried it anyway. "Imagine the boxes unpacked," her friend said. "Imagine everything in your office already in its place. Do this for a few days. Don't try to unpack. Just sit on your porch with a glass of lemonade and imagine." So Bertha decided to give it a try. (It had to be better than tackling all those boxes.) Every day she'd sit outside on her porch with a tall glass of lemonade, close her eyes, and envision her office already in perfect order, every single thing in its place. To her surprise, the exercise was easy. And it felt good. Then the strangest thing happened. By the end of the week, she became so excited by her vision that she started to unpack. The hours flew by. The task flowed naturally. And it turned out to be fun, because rather than thinking the whole time of how she didn't want her office to look, she was inspired by the vision of how she did want it to be.

When it comes to organizing any area in our life, the first thing we need to do is envision, in our mind's eye, what we want. If it's an organized closet, we need to imagine opening the door to that closet and gasping with relief at how incredibly ordered and beautiful it looks. Envision freshly painted walls, beautiful brass hooks, and colorful boxes with lids, all clearly labeled and neatly lined up on shelf after shelf. We also need to feel how wonderful that imaginary scenario is. Feeling is a key part of envisioning.

Remember: Organization does not begin with long, frantically scribbled to-do lists on yellow legal pads. It begins with relaxing and using your imagination to create a clear, joyful vision of what you want in your life.

EXERCISE

Light a candle, close your eyes, and spend five minutes imagining what your new, organized, clutter-free life looks or feels like. Don't worry if you can't visualize it in perfect detail, just make sure to really feel the happiness, relief, accomplishment, and ease you'll get from being more organized. Let this exercise be easy and relaxing, completely without strain. Some people see things in their mind's eye while others receive more of a feeling sense in their bodies. Try this envisioning exercise for five minutes each day this month, and see what it inspires.

Assess

Tom's office was a mess. When he looked at it, all he saw was massive amounts of disorganization. He didn't have a clue what to do. "It's a wreck," he told his colleague Margaret. "I'm hopeless." Margaret laughed and offered to help. She walked slowly around his office, studying specific areas: his crowded one-drawer file cabinet and his messy bookshelves spilling over with books, magazines, and manuals. Then she stopped by the large picture window. "What works in this office," she began, "is that you have a really nice space with a great window that gives you lots of light. And you've got plenty of room in here." Tom felt instantly relieved. "But what's not working," she added, "is that you need a larger file cabinet. Buy at least a two-drawer, maybe even a four-drawer. This way you can expand." Then she pointed to his bookshelf. "Too many books and magazines crowded onto too little shelf space," she said. "That's why it doesn't work. Either dump some publications or get a larger bookcase. Then you won't have any trouble being neat." Tom looked at her in amazement. "How did you do that?" he asked. "I thought this place was a total disaster." Margaret smiled. "I just focused on specifics. When you do that, you can always find a solution."

Once you've clarified and envisioned the life you want, you can begin to assess your situation to start determining what you will need to do to get there. You'll want to make sure your assessments are specific. A general statement like, "My house is a total pigsty," just amplifies feelings of overwhelm and shame. Instead, try to zero in on one concrete problem at a time and brainstorm how to fix it. For example: "I have a small bathroom, with only one shelf and medicine cabinet, but I have tons of half-used hair products, expired prescriptions, and other rarely used items piled everywhere."

You may also want to assess which habits lead to your disorganization. For instance, if you always overbook and then cancel appointments at the last minute, is it because you have a habit of saying "yes" when you really want to say "no"? If you come home at the end of the day and throw your clothes on the floor, is it because you're too exhausted from not taking care of yourself to hang them up?

Pam Young, author of *Sidetracked Home Executives: From Pigpen to Paradise,* suggests that you try to "Look at your mess with new eyes, as if company were coming over." She even suggests putting a "for sale" sign on your front lawn "to get you into the mindset of 'What are they going to think?'"

Don't forget to take equal note of everything you're doing well. "Most people know what doesn't work in their lives," emphasizes declutter coach Marilyn Nagel. So it's equally important, she says, to assess what does work. Perhaps your car is a mess, but your checkbook is balanced. Or maybe you can never find a matching pair of socks, but you're always on time. Assess the full picture, and give yourself full credit for your strengths.

EXERCISE

Take a tour of your home, your office, and your schedule. With pad in hand, investigate your closets, drawers, cabinets, desk, basement, garage, address books, e-mail in-box, and calendars. Pick specific areas that need help. Then begin by asking yourself: What works in this area of my home or life? What doesn't work and why? What resources do I need to solve my problems? And what habits are contributing to my disorganization? Then go further by working with the following questions suggested by Marilyn Nagel: What's causing the specific problem? What's preventing the solution? What do I have actually have room for? What am I willing to let go of?

As you complete your assessment, notice and record any uncomfortable feelings, physical sensations, thoughts, or excuses that come up. In the next chapter, "Feel," we'll look at how to address your emotional reactions to your assessment, so that they don't prevent you from getting organized.

Feel

This was the day, John decided, when he was finally going to clean out the garage. After making himself a strong cup of coffee, he marched into the crammed space, which was overflowing with everything from rusted wheelbarrows and broken ladders to half-open paint cans and collections of *National Geographic*. As he scanned the mess, he noticed a knot tightening in the pit of his stomach: *I'm such a jerk. How could I let it get this bad? What's wrong with me anyway? I'm a sloppy good-for-nothing!*

Gritting his teeth, he forced himself to look at different areas in the garage. In one corner he noticed piles of art supplies, Christmas decorations, and Halloween costumes that his wife never put away. *She's the real clutter bug. She's the one who messes up the garage with all her unfinished projects and broken promises.* Then he noticed his son's sports equipment spilled everywhere. *If it wasn't for everyone else in the family, I could be neater!* Completely pissed off, he stormed out of the garage, grabbed a beer, and turned on the television. The garage continued to be a mess.

According to psychologists and organizational experts, John's reaction to his garage is absolutely normal and perfectly human. Feelings of shame and guilt are probably the most common obstacles we face when we decide to organize some aspect of our lives. "People see their clutter as a failure," says Cindy Glovinsky, a psychotherapist and author of *Making Peace with the Things in Your Life.* "They see themselves as failures. They become paralyzed by shame." Almost every client Glovinsky has worked with eventually admits how ashamed they feel.

What complicates matters is that before we can even get to our feelings of shame and guilt, they're often obscured by blame. Blaming someone else feels better—and less painful—than blaming ourselves. "People often personify their things and get a sense that the things are doing something to them," explains Glovinsky. We feel victimized by our stuff, offering excuses like, "That new day planner I purchased isn't working," or "The papers on my desk keep piling up no matter how much I do," or "My closets are just too small." We offer up all kinds of explanations to obscure our deep, uncomfortable feelings of shame, guilt, fear, and insecurity. But eventually, we have to acknowledge the truth. "You have to recognize," says Glovinsky, "that people make clutter. Things don't make clutter."

So a critical step in beginning to organize any area of your life is to admit that you are struggling and to allow yourself to feel the pain that this struggle causes you. We need to gently but courageously acknowledge the areas in our life that need more attention and the painful feelings and judgments that come with that acknowledgment. Because until we do, we'll just keep resorting to avoidance and blame, and our garages and our lives will remain a mess.

EXERCISE

In the last chapter, you took a thorough assessment of your home, your office, and your calendar to uncover where you would like to be better organized. Choose one of those areas now, and revisit it. Review the emotions, judgments, and physical sensations that came up. Give yourself five or ten minutes to face the feelings and disturbing judgments. Don't turn away from them. Instead lean into them with curiosity and compassion.

Many of us fear that facing our feelings will be overwhelming. But in fact, facing them so actually releases them. And allows us to move forward. So let your feelings run their course. Relax into the shame or fear or guilt. Feelings don't mean you're weak or wrong. They just mean we're human. Just acknowledge the situation and how you feel. And remember to honor your genuine desire and efforts to change.

Confess

Last night, I had a horrible dream. I was squeezed inside my jam-packed bedroom closet, staring at the mass of tangled clothing: A flowered Hawaiian muumuu, two sizes too small, that I bought eleven years ago on vacation; a glittery, slinky purple pants outfit I wore once at a business conference back in 1993; half-a-dozen embroidered sweaters, slightly too big, that I inherited from my now-dead mother, who had bought them one night during a QVC marathon. Suddenly a fierce-looking policewoman burst into the closet, handcuffed me, and screeched, "You're under arrest!" Instantly, we were transported to an enormous courtroom flooded with white light. A judge with intimidating bushy eyebrows glowered down at me from on high. "Do you swear to tell the truth, the whole truth, and nothing but the truth?!" he bellowed. "The truth about what, your honor?" I stammered. He roared back, "About all the clothes in your closet that you haven't worn in years!!!" I woke up, drenched in sweat, and vowed to donate everything that didn't fit anymore.

19

This dream illustrates one of the most important principles of organizing any area of your life, says clutter consultant Michele Passoff: Telling the truth. By wholeheartedly confessing to yourself the truth about your clutter and disorganization, you become liberated from the past and make room for the present. For instance, how often are you late for meetings? Do you schedule a dentist appointment at nine thirty and then a breakfast meeting at ten fifteen, only to arrive forty minutes late? "Tell the truth about how long it will take you to get there," urges Passoff. "Don't schedule time consistent with your wishes; schedule it realistically."

Same goes for those sewing projects taking up half of your closet. Are you ever really going to make that two-piece dress? Are you ever really going to use those scrapbooks to organize your family photos? Confess the truth. Once you do, you'll be free to take action: hire someone to organize those photos; buy a dress if you don't actually enjoy making them; donate those skin-tight skirts to Goodwill so you can accept your body now. "The curious paradox," the humanistic psychologist Carl Rogers once wrote, "is that when I accept myself just as I am then I can change." That's the power behind telling the truth. Only by confessing, from the heart, will you open up the space, sometimes literally, for something new to enter.

EXERCISE

Head to an area that haunts you the most and tell the truth out loud. Stand in front of your files and confess that you have no intention of ever finishing that twenty-year-old screenplay; go to your garage and confess that you're never going to rewire that ugly yard-sale lamp or build that model airplane. Looking at your busy calendar, confess that you really never liked your former coworker in the first place and you need to cancel that lunch date with him. But remember, while confessing is liberating, it can also trigger feelings of sadness or loss. So take a few minutes to breath into any uncomfortable feelings. And know that telling the truth will set you free.

Personalize

In preparation for writing this book, I started to organize my desk and files. At the time, this meant shuffling piles from here to there, opening drawers, staring inside, feeling overwhelmed, and then going out for a vanilla latte. One morning, on the way back from my latte run, I bumped into my next-door neighbor. Instead of borrowing a cup of sugar, I borrowed her organized brain. She and her husband have three small children yet their house is very, very neat. She stood at my desk, looked at my pencil cup with its dozens of pens and pencils (many of which no longer worked), and said, sweetly but firmly, "Keep only three pens on your desk, dump the ones that don't work, and put any extras inside your desk drawer."

So, after two decades of crowded artsy pencil cups, I switched to hiding my writing implements in my drawer. She also helped me label my files clearly and put them neatly inside a file cabinet (I had kept them in plain view). I thanked her and she left. Then the oddest thing began to happen. The longer I sat at my newly ordered desk, the more uncomfortable I became. Where were all my pens? Where were all the papers that sat on my desk? Where were my files? I felt too far away from them. Not being able to see them made me sweat. What's wrong with me? I thought. Am I organizationally challenged?

"Absolutely not!" laughed Lee Silber, author of *Organizing from the Right Side of the Brain*. He proceeded to explain that I'm simply a right-brainer, a creative type who is visually oriented. Right-brain people need to see things, he says, so "putting it away in a file or drawer means it's as good as lost."

According to Silber, left-brain folks like to be in control of everything, especially their environment. They especially like to compartmentalize, finish things, and put things away. "At the end of the day," says Silber, "they always clean off their desk." Society, Silber passionately points out, tries to force people to be more left-brain, insisting that neatness and punctuality is paramount. "The problem with most books about organizing," he emphasizes, "is that they all focus on only one way to do things—a left-brain approach—an approach that is very linear and structured." But he explains that the logical, linear approach is not realistic at all for right-brainers.

Rather than trying to squeeze ourselves into systems that don't work for us, we can adopt Silber's more personalized approach: "You don't have to change who you are to be organized." Sure you want to be efficient enough to function. But the idea is to become aware of your own unique patterns and approaches to doing things. For example, most organizing experts agree that bulletin boards are clutter magnets.

Silber disagrees, explaining that right-brain people should have numerous bulletin boards. Organizing books also proclaim, "File don't pile," but Silber declares that for right-brainers, it's more effective to "pile with a purpose."

So allow yourself to personalize all organization tips to fit your natural style. If paper piles work for you, make neater piles that are labeled clearly and leave them on your desk. Instead of trying to change your messy habit of cluttering the kitchen counter with keys, coins, and crumpled receipts, place a pretty bowl there to catch the contents of your pockets. "Pay attention to where you put things," emphasizes Silber. "Generally that's where you want them to go. There's actually a method to your messiness. The goal is to find your own style, to become a better you, not a different you."

EXERCISE

As a first step to personalizing you own organizational approach, review the areas of home, work, and time, and consider whether you're more of a right-brainer or a left-brainer in each of those areas. Remember, left-brainers are more logical, analytical, objective, and rational; they always arrive right on time (they can't stand people who don't), neatly fold their underwear and socks, hate messy desks and homes, and keep their pencils lined up in perfect order. Right-brainers are more intuitive, emotional, creative, random, and subjective; they get so caught up in the moment, they often forget completely about time; they enjoy piles of papers on their desk (and know precisely what's in them), and feel suffocated when they walk into a perfectly organized, mess-free home.

Breathe

Janet was late for her daughter's play. She raced out of the house, grabbed the mail, turned on her cell phone, and nibbled a sandwich. By the time she reached the school, she'd checked her voice mail, returned calls, scribbled down notes and appointments in her day planner, and eaten the rest of lunch. The play had already started, so she slipped quietly into the back row. Every time she tried to focus on the stage, she'd get distracted by new concerns. Had she forgotten to tell the landscaper about the roses? Was she supposed to pick up the birthday cake for Bill's surprise party? Would that new client approve her proposal? On the way home from school, her daughter excitedly fired questions at her: "Did you like the scenery, mommy? Wasn't it funny when Quinn forgot his lines? What did you think of my costume?" Suddenly Janet realized she had scheduled an important meeting on the wrong day. As she fumbled through her notes, her daughter repeated, "Mommy, didn't you like my costume?" Janet stared at her little girl suddenly, realizing she couldn't recall a single detail of what her daughter had worn.

"In this day and age, people's lives are filled with so much stress and activities," says Kathleen Thurston, a Buddhist meditation instructor and feng shui consultant. "We actually think that multitasking is an asset. Yet it's just another way of creating distractions for ourselves. Doing so many things at once makes it difficult to focus." In fact, recent studies have found that our performance is compromised, not enhanced, when we do more than one complex activity at a time.

"The mind is so filled with distracting thoughts," says Thurston. "We feel overwhelmed. It's like mental clutter." Buddhists aptly call this state "monkey-mind"—the annoying, undisciplined tendency for our minds to get distracted, jumping from thought to thought, like chattering monkeys swinging from trees. And since research suggests that the average person thinks thousands of thoughts per day, the big question is: When you collapse on your couch after work, are you exhausted from of how busy you physically were, or from the relentless, unfocused activity of your mind?

Being able to slow down and focus on what we're doing in the moment, whether it's chopping carrots or listening to another person talk, is a key component to putting our lives in order.

"Slowing down is the only way we can access something greater than our own egos," says life coach Jennifer Louden, author of *The Woman's Comfort Book*. "When we move quickly, we block our ability to know anything more than what we know. We try to organize from our minds only—

and our minds are not able to know what the best use of our time is. Our hearts know, but we can't access that when are moving fast."

As you slow down and give your attention to one thing at a time, not only does that calm you, but it subdues the tornado of thoughts spiraling through your brain. That's the essence of breathing meditation—training the monkey-mind to follow the rhythm of the breath. "By just focusing on the in and out of the breath," says Thurston, "we can develop the mind muscle of concentration."

The less distracted we are, the happier we become. And a happier mind makes for a kinder human being, transforming us, Thurston says, into, "someone who can make wiser choices in life." Since all the experts agree that making good choices is the key to a more organized life, the simple act of slowing down promises enormous long-term benefits.

EXERCISE

Mindfulness can be practiced anywhere and any time—even while you're organizing a linen closet, decluttering a junk drawer, filing papers, or planning your week. As you pick up an object, consciously slow your physical movement; notice how the pen looks and feels in your hand. As you sit down, feel the leather chair beneath you; notice the smooth grain of the conference table and how it looks in the light. Give all your attention to what's right in front of you. You can also stop for a few moments and begin watching your breath. See if you can count ten consecutive breaths without your mind wandering off. When you do drift off, gently refocus by saying "Count," and return to your breath. As you return to your original activity, allow yourself to bring that calm focus to the task in front of you.

Reward

Kelly kept avoiding tackling the mess in her home office. Every time she'd begin sorting through the papers on her desk, she'd end up spacing out by reading a magazine. Fortunately, she stumbled across a great article about using rewards as a form of motivation. She decided to work in her office for three hours and then treat herself to a low-fat frozen yogurt. But about forty-five minutes into the task, she got so frustrated, she gave up, and binged on an entire bag of peanut M&Ms. How come rewarding herself didn't work?

Because the reward, says life coach Marilyn Nagel, has to be worth it. "We've got to have a carrot at the end of the stick," she explains, "when it comes to doing tasks or taking on projects that we resist." The bigger the reward, the better, she insists, and the motivation or incentive should always be pleasurable. Also make sure to avoid using punishing "shoulds" instead of rewards—telling yourself you should organize the garage because your in-laws are coming is not going to inspire you to leap up and begin. But if straightening the garage means you can play with your new watercolors when you've finished, that's real motivation.

Nagel also suggests getting your friends in on the reward game; for instance, tell your tennis partner that you can only play on Saturday if you finish decluttering the kitchen junk drawer before then. Another idea is to make organizing the basement a fun family event by going out to a movie together when it's done.

Sometimes when facing a particularly daunting task, we may need continual rewards sprinkled throughout the activity. In this case, break the larger goal into minitasks and sandwich in several fun rewards. For example, if you've decided on two hours of cleaning that you're not particularly looking forward to, sandwich in brief rewards every thirty minutes: a cup of tea, a long-distance call to a friend, a stroll around the block.

As great as rewards can be, author Jennifer Louden cautions that focusing only on the eventual reward without taking any pleasure in the task can be counterproductive: "When we think of rewards, we often are thinking of what we deserve to get us through the pain of what we don't want to do. That can often lead to shadow comforts, such as overeating, watching too much TV, surfing the Internet mindlessly." So make sure, says Louden, that when you choose your rewards, they nourish and support you, rather than undermining your progress. "Also think about what is intrinsically valuable about what you're doing," she adds. "If you're decluttering, consider what is rewarding about that intrinsically—and that will lead you toward a cherry-on-the-top thinking."

Make a list of thirty-one small rewards you'd love to receive for completing any organizing, decluttering, or time management task. For example: receiving a foot massage, buying a bouquet of tulips, spending time on a hobby you love, or indulging in an afternoon nap. Then one by one, give yourself a reward each time you read one of these chapters and complete an exercise! Pay attention to how the reward feels in comparison to the task. Does it feel nourishing and pleasurable enough? Is it truly motivating? When you make your list, try to make your rewards ones that are genuinely fulfilling and pleasurable. Then, when actually completing a task, contemplate the intrinsic value of completing that task, and allow that to be part of your reward.

Simplify

The Art and Science of Creating Order

*"Out of clutter, find simplicity. From discord, find harmony.
In the middle of difficulty lies opportunity."*

—ALBERT EINSTEIN

Now that you are clearer about this whole organizing thing and what it means to you in your own life, it's time to skip on down to the water's edge, and dive in! In this section, you'll face and work with the clutter and disorganization that exists in your home or office. But trust me, getting organized is nowhere near as scary as you think. The experts I interviewed offered lots of wonderful suggestions and words of wisdom. And I promise the steps to simplifying your home or office are fun, simple, and, in the end, empowering.

Commit

Joanne walked into her house armed with bags of books. She'd just spent hours at the library, determined to conquer, once and for all, her lifestyle of disorganization. She set the books neatly down on her coffee table, made a cup of tea, and began reading.

Three weeks later, Joanne was still reading and her house was still a mess. Added to the pile of library books were now a dozen new books and magazines on decluttering and time management that she'd purchased from the bookstore along with promising audio and video courses. By the time her mother called two months later to ask how the organizing was going, all Joanne could do was stare despairingly at her cluttered coffee table. She realized she hadn't taken a single action to making things more organized.

Perhaps if Joanne had followed the advice of Nike, the renowned sports company, she would have made better progress. Because when it comes to taking action, Nike's world-famous ad campaign leaves absolutely no wiggle room: Just do it!

We can rationalize putting things off for weeks or spend months intending to begin, but Nike's no-nonsense motto is like a sobering splash of ice water. At some point, we have to commit. According to Webster, to commit means "to carry into action deliberately." It's time now for you to make that commitment and take action.

If these words have you shaking in your disorganized boots, you're not alone. Barry Izsak, board president of the National Association of Professional Organizers, explains that "People don't know where to start. They're afraid to begin." His solution? "Start somewhere."

A good place to start is by making an actual appointment to follow through, says declutter coach Marilyn Nagel. "Everyone has a calendar. Make an appointment with yourself, just like a doctor's appointment." She warns against getting bogged down in the how-to. So for every minute you spend reading this book, make sure you're spending at least two doing actual organization.

Once you make a commitment, you'll have to keep it. Nagel emphasizes that follow through isn't always easy. "Research shows that we're not wired to follow through," she says, "were not like squirrels collecting nuts." So avoid getting too squirrelly, then, Nagel suggests finding an accountability partner. Look for someone who also wants to get organized, or at least wants to support you in doing so. Ideally, you'd find someone who will truly expect you to follow through. "Be accountable," says Nagel, "to someone you would not risk disappointing or displeasing, someone who is a little outside your immediate family."

Once you've committed to a specific, doable decluttering

task or organizational activity, keep the promise. If you need help staying on task, set a timer for thirty minutes to keep you on track. Or, if you tend to break promises too easily, invite people over to your house on a specific date, Nagel suggests. When you know people are coming for dinner or a visit, it can motivate you to accomplish what you agreed to do, such as decluttering the family room or living room. Whether it's a monthly poker game, a weekly women's group, or just a dinner party, once you schedule the gathering at your house, you're more likely to take action because if you don't people will actually see the existing mess and disorder.

EXERCISE

Pick your first organizing task. Choose something small and achievable, such as decluttering a junk drawer, bookshelf, medicine cabinet, jewelry box, glove compartment, or wallet. For greater satisfaction, choose something that's really been bugging you. Then pick a time within the next twenty-four hours to complete the task, schedule it in your calendar, decide how long you'll spend, and tell someone else your plan. When your scheduled appointment time comes, do the task. Once you're done, give your accountability partner a call to report your success, give yourself a nice reward, and commit and schedule three more small, doable tasks to do in the next week.

Reduce

Here are some things that have taken up space in my home (and, be honest, probably your home too): Unused pasta machines and hand blenders purchased at fundraisers; thigh masters, Tony Robbins personal power CDs, and self-help books never read; shoes; rusted lamps, rusted tools, rusted screws; shoes; chipped china from relatives I don't really like; souvenir thimbles, ashtrays, and mugs from places once visited with ex-lovers; shoes; antiquated skis, tennis rackets and scuba gear; tangled fishing poles and jump ropes; expensive exercise equipment that hasn't felt my sweat in years; dusty plastic flowers; shoes; faded photos of people whose names I can't remember; out-of-date eyeglasses, medications, and make-up; expired canned goods; mini-shampoo bottles from less-than-five-star hotels; stained tablecloths; shoes; wooden plaques and three-foot-tall trophies won for something absurdly unimportant; suitcases with rusted zippers; obsolete computer parts; stacks of books and magazines rivaling the Empire State building; unmatched socks; shoes.

Our stuff. It's the symptom of a cultural disease, declares Don Aslett, author of *Clutter's Last Stand;* a contemporary phenomenon intensified by the 24/7 onslaught of media and advertising, brainwashing us to believe that "more is better." This never-ending flood of misguided messages shows up everywhere: television, movie theatres, shopping networks, magazines, billboards, junk mail, and e-mail spam. Forget global warming—Western civilization is doomed to melt beneath the heat of its own passionate consumerism.

Professional organizer Barry Izsak concurs. "Consumers are bombarded by the media. And the predominant message is get more stuff. We have more disposable income than ever, and we obey. We run out and buy all this stuff without thinking where we're going to put it or how we are going to use it."

And when we run out of room, we pay someone else to store it. According to the Self Storage Association, a not-for-profit trade group, one out of every eleven American households pays for self-storage space, an increase of fifty percent in the past decade. And while it took the self-storage industry twenty-five years to build its first billion square feet of storage space, they added the second billion square feet of space in just eight years.

Aslett calls these self-storage units "junk bunkers!" Insurance agents have reported that when storage units burn down or get robbed, most of their clients can't even remember what's inside. "People are uncomfortable with empty space," Aslett adds. "They have to fill it."

Practically speaking, the first step is to "live appropriate to your space," according to consultant Michelle Passoff. If you've got fifteen-hundred square feet of possessions and only eight-hundred square feet of apartment, it's not time to pay for storage; it's time to reduce. In our quest to simplify our lives, we need to get comfortable living with more space. It might be scary at first but in the end, it feels wonderful.

In addition to reducing what you already own, you'll also want to reduce what you buy. Each time you're about to purchase something new, whether it's a knickknack that catches your fancy or something that seems like an utter necessity, Aslett insists there's only one burning question to ask yourself: Does this enhance my life?

Reducing also involves a shift in perspective and in values. "People think things will make them happy," Aslett explains, But a lifestyle of clutter, says Aslett, "isolates us from love and affection." There are really only two things in life that count, he asserts: "To love and be loved. And too much stuff gets in the way."

EXERCISE

Reducing means having less and living more. So for the next week, go on a buying diet. Purchase only absolute necessities. What's a necessity? Ask yourself Aslett's question: Will this item enhance my life? If your answer is yes, enact the twenty-four-hour rule: Wait a day. If you still really want it and you really believe it will serve a positive purpose in your life, then take it home. As you go through the week, keep a record of everything you considered buying, and how it felt to either buy or not buy it. Pay attention to the thoughts and emotions that arise. Deciding not to buy the latest CD or that garden gnome might feel sad or even scary. But as you relax into the experience, you may also find that it's a relief not to buy so much. And you may discover the quiet joy of being content with what you have ... and who you are.

Purge

I couldn't stand it any more. Every single time I opened my office closet I felt like screaming. I had a file cabinet packed full of half-completed book projects, ancient journals filled with teenage angst, and unfinished articles from as far back as the late seventies. Shoved in a corner were shopping bags of my mother's stuff that I kept after she died—her jewelry and house keys, photos of her friends, and all kinds of other things from her daily life that I couldn't bear to look at. I had drafts of books that were already published and a pair of giant fairy wings made of feathers that kept shedding. So one weekend, when I was feeling brave, I started purging. I tossed drafts of manuscripts that were already published, dumped ancient files full of notes from the early eighties, donated some of my mom's jewelry to a local community theatre group, and gave the fairy wings to a little girl next door. When it was all over, I felt so much lighter, as if I had been in a marathon therapy session, as if I had faced my past ... and moved on.

Katherine Thurston, author of *Taking the Sacred Path Home: Applying the Ancient Wisdom of Feng Shui,* points out that purging can free us of our attachments to the past. By holding onto our old clutter, she says, there's no room for anything new to enter, and it keeps our thoughts, emotions, and energy trapped in yesterday. Energetically, my office closet was literally pulling me backward in time, back to all those old, crusty writing projects, back to all my past unresolved issues.

"Clutter creates disharmony," Thurston explains. "Most of the time, it's outdated, like wearing seventies clothes. It keeps us in the past, not current with who we are and what we need now. It restricts and confuses our possibilities." Purging is so important, she says, because "it helps us get clear about what our intentions are for our life."

Thurston suggests that we approach our space—every room in our home—as if it were a sacred space. "Think of the highest spiritual person you admire coming to visit you. That's the way we should create our home." Our space should not be ordinary or mundane, she emphasizes, "It should actually uplift and inspire us." Thurston suggests we ask ourselves, "Do I love it or use it? Does it have heart? If it doesn't fulfill these requirements," she says, "then it's not serving us."

But be aware of your moods. If you're feeling particularly sentimental or vulnerable, it may not be the best time to purge. Wait until you're enthusiastic and energetic about moving forward with your life, or until you're feeling angry that your stuff is holding you back.

Once you get the initial purge done, you may want to choose a weekend twice a year, perhaps in spring and autumn, when "It feels natural to enter into another wave of purging, cleaning, and clearing." The physical act of clearing clutter, Thurston adds, will also initiate the process of clearing your mental, emotional, and spiritual clutter: "It's amazing how liberating it feels."

"Learn to enjoy this process of elimination," says Thurston, "because you will find it a continuous one of editing your belongings to stay current with your need for harmony, growth, and authenticity."

EXERCISE

This weekend, take a block of time to purge. Thurston suggests renting a debris box from the sanitation department. They'll drop it off in your driveway and pick it up one week later. "You can really get rid of a lot of stuff, including furniture." If a debris box doesn't seem right, follow Thurston's Three Giant Black Garbage Bags Rule. Get three black garbage bags and spend the weekend filling them with the stuff you no longer need or want. Good places to start are the refrigerator and freezer, pantries, medicine cabinets, and supply closets, which often get jam-packed with old, unnecessary, or broken items. Focus this first round of purging on things that are damaged or clearly not wanted by you or anyone else, and give them the old heave-ho!

Sort

Timmy had trouble finding the toys he wanted to play with because they were lost in piles scattered all over his bedroom. If he wanted to play with his favorite Batman figurine, he didn't know where to look. So his dad purchased a children's shelving unit that held ten colored bins. Timmy sat down with his dad and together they began separating the massive piles into ten categories: Plastic army guys, superhero figurines, and Disney characters went into a people pile; undersea animals, horses, and dinosaurs into the creature pile; stones and crystals into the rock collection pile; rubber balls of all sizes into the "bounce" pile; cars, trucks, boats, planes, and trains into "vehicles." Then there were the puzzle pile, puppets pile, musical instruments pile, and "????" pile. As they sorted, they created two additional categories "throw-away" for broken toys, and "give-away" for toys he'd outgrown. When they finished, Timmy felt great because now he knew exactly where to find everything. And his dad felt great because now Timmy knew where to put things away as well.

Sorting and categorizing your stuff is the next important step in organizing. But trying to sort through things without dumping everything out of its space will inevitably lead to failure, says Don Aslett. So first choose your project: a closet, set of drawers, bookshelf, or cabinet. Then get four boxes and label them "keep," "toss," "donate," and "undecided." Finally, take everything out of the space in question and put each item into one of those boxes. Yes, folks, that means emptying your entire linen closet onto the floor, or dumping all the contents of your junk drawer onto your kitchen table.

If most of the stuff you're sorting keeps landing in the "keep" box, contemplate the wisdom offered by Marilyn Nagel: Your real attachment is not to that funky ceramic planter Aunt Tillie made you; it's to your Aunt Tillie! So instead of keeping the item, try tossing it into the "undecided" box. When you do, says Nagel, "It begins to break the bond between you and that thing." In other words, just the act of considering not keeping something you've had a great emotional attachment to begins to create some space. Keep one "undecided box" in your house that you revisit every six months. This can gently allow you to release your intense attachments to things. (If it helps, take a photo of your mother's china before sending it off to charity.)

Olympic swimmer Anthony Irvin eloquently illustrated how people and experiences are more important than objects when he donated his gold medal to raise funds for the Asian tsunami victims. "The medal itself is just a symbol of the work I put in," he said, "but the work and time I invested, I still have that. That dedication and tenacity and trying to pursue things with excellence—still have that." In other words, as Aslett says, "Keep it in your heart, not your closet!"

Don't know how to decide whether to toss something out? Ask yourself: Do I feel really good having this or does it bring me down? Does it add to my feeling of space and hope for the future, or does it leave me feeling heavy and burdened?

Ultimately, it's up to you to decide what you enjoy keeping around and what you don't. While Aslett maintains that the excuse "but I can use it someday" is a rationalization to hold on to clutter, Lee Silber, author of *Organizing from the Right Side of the Brain,* disagrees. When a creative, right-brain person insists they can use something, says Silber, they actually mean it. That rusted carrot peeler from your Polish grandmother really could end up in a sculpture someday, or as inspiration for that memoir, or as a prop in your play. Sorting isn't about giving up who you are; it's about creating space for you to let go and thrive.

Once you've sorted, it's time to categorize by grouping like items together. In other words, group canned goods together, boxed goods together, skirts together, and suits together. Depending on how much of a left-brainer you are, you may enjoy breaking categories down further, such as grouping canned vegetables together, canned soups together, boxed cereals together, and so on. But don't go that far unless it feels good—this isn't about earning an A+, it's about making your life easier. "You don't have to come up with perfect categories," Silber adds. Goofy categories are fine, too, he says, if they work for you. And remember that they can be changed as needed.

If you're struggling with what categories to create, visit a bookstore, supermarket, or hardware store to see how they categorize items, suggests June Saruwatari, The Organizing Maniac™. "But if you want to go deeper," she says, "then organize based on who you are and how you see the world." According to Saruwatari, categorizing is ultimately about "honoring the way you use a particular item." For instance, she loves making sandwiches, so she groups all the sandwich stuff (deli meats and condiments) in one place in her fridge. Likewise, you could decide to group your groceries by the meals they're intended for, so that when it comes time to cook, you know exactly where to go.

As you engage in this process, be easy with yourself. This is not about creating stress or unhappiness! Many experts suggest designating a junk drawer in your home where you can toss those sentimental bottle caps, ticket stubs, single earrings, and half-used batteries. A little junk keeps you real, and gently reminds you that ultimately life is messy.

EXERCISE

The time has come to pick a larger project, like a closet or a room. Clearly label your boxes "keep," "toss," "donate," and "undecided." Set a timer, turn on your favorite music, and sort! Keep a pad nearby so you can jot down inspired categories or themes for your keep box. In a later chapter, "Contain," you'll learn how to store all those categorized items neatly and beautifully distinguished.

Consolidate

Whenever anyone walked into Teddy's apartment they were startled to see a huge collection of travel memorabilia. Shelves were filled with thimbles, silver spoons, ceramic bells, mugs, and ashtrays proving that Teddy had visited every state park, amusement park, and travel destination in America. It's not that the souvenirs weren't fun to look at, it's that they took up almost every bit of space in his one-bedroom apartment. When close friends suggested he let go of some of it, he refused. "These remind me of all the good times I've had with my ex-girlfriend. I never want to forget a single place or moment," he'd protest. "I can't let go of them!"

Sometimes our attachments to things are extremely difficult to release. Whether it's trinkets and knickknacks left to us as part of our inheritance from family and beloved relatives or souvenirs and memorabilia from ex-lovers, old friends, or past chapters of our lives, these objects can serve as reminders of who we once were. But what do we do when these mementos are taking up all of our space in the present and not leaving room for new memories?

In *Clutter's Last Stand,* Don Aslett shares a unique strategy: "It's perhaps a compromise, but miniaturizing is a solution especially suited to keepsakes and sentimental items-sort of a 'reduce-it-if-you-must-keep-it' strategy."

What he and other experts suggest is that rather than keeping all items with sentimental value, you "miniaturize" your collections by taking photos of the majority of the items, putting those photos in scrapbooks, and then getting rid of the items themselves. This way you can hold onto your mementos but let go of physical clutter. This is a great idea if you have lots of trophies or other bulky items taking up room. Miniaturizing doesn't mean you can't keep anything; simply look over your collections, pick a few pieces that you love the most, and let go of the rest. You may want to frame the few items you keep in a beautiful shadow box—or otherwise highlight them in your home—to remind you of the person or event they represent.

I once went on a fairy-statue collecting binge. I had dozens of cute, adorable, dust-collecting fairy and elf knick-knacks. They were everywhere. After writing this book, I chose the six I loved most, displayed them on a small shelf, and gave the rest away. I actually found that I enjoy the remaining statues more now that there are just a precious few.

EXERCISE

What needs to be condensed in your home or office? Look over your collections and the sentimental stuff you're holding on to. Decide what's really important to you, keep only your very favorites, and let go of anything that reminds you negative experiences. If it helps, take a few photos of the items that didn't make the cut and put them in a scrapbook. Then donate or recycle the items you no longer need. And enjoy the new space that's now open for fresh memories.

Contain

One of my favorite greeting cards is by illustrator Mary Engelbreit. It shows a little boy hugging his adorable black-and-white puppy. Beneath the artwork, Engelbreit's simple message underscores the sentiment: "Everybody needs their own Spot." The same is true in organizing. Everything you have, everything you're ever going to buy, needs its own spot, its own distinct home. My fantasy is that Engelbreit's art studio is beautifully ordered with colorful containers, jars, and hat boxes everywhere.

I know for a fact that Marilyn Radzat, another successful artist, really does put everything in its own spot. Her wildly creative ocean-front studio is a delight to behold. As a renowned sculptor and doll artist whose costumed pieces sell in galleries around the country, she has an endless array of tools and materials. Everything she uses, from colored sea glass and exotic mosaics to antique fabrics and hand-made beads have their own special homes. Ceramic mugs and vases hold paintbrushes, scissors, and sculpting tools; beautiful bowls individually display shells, jewels, stones, and one-of-a-kind buttons. Everything is ordered and accessible. "The container is not just a means to an end," says Radzat. "The container and what's inside work together synergistically. My containers are contexts that add to what I'm containing and become sources of inspiration. The rhinestones I place in a blue glass bowl become more. The container enhances what I'm storing."

June Saruwatari, cohost of TLC's *Home Made Simple,* concurs: "'Containerizing' is about honoring the way you live your life." Choosing the containers can become a way to express your creativity, she adds: "It's what makes your life a work of art."

But don't go on a buying spree yet. Once you've sorted and categorized, assess what size containers you'll need. It's too easy to spend hundreds of dollars on elegant hat boxes and antique suitcases, only to bring them home and discover they're not the right size.

"In the beginning, until you understand how important organizing is to the quality of your life," suggests Saruwatari, "begin with shoeboxes and boxes, just so you can see how easy life can be and how it can flow." Then you can start exploring containers. "Buy something that makes you feel alive and speaks to you." It's a great opportunity, she says, "to discover who you are, what you like, what colors, images, and textures really inspire you."

But choosing containers isn't just about aesthetics, says Lee Silber, author of *Organizing from the Right Side of the Brain.* It's also about your natural thinking style. For right-brainers, containers that allow you to see what's inside is critical, he says. So if you're right-brained (that is, if you tend to be creative, sensitive, visual, intuitive, or emotional) choose see-through plastic boxes, glass jars, nets, hooks, bulletin boards, wine racks, or milk crates. Or at least label everything clearly. "Label-makers can be fun," adds Silber.

The idea of containing can be expanded to include specific zones in your house. For example, you might designate the hallway closet for sports equipment, jackets, and umbrellas only; the living room for reading, movies, and music only; and the home office for all electronic gadgets, and computer paraphernalia. With this kind of system, when a DVD lands on the dining table or a soccer ball rolls into the bathroom, you'll know just where to return it.

And remember that the most frequently used stuff should always be the easiest to access. Whether you're organizing your office supply closet or your fridge, decide what you reach for most often and make sure those items are right up front.

Bottom line, emphasizes Silber: "Not knowing where to put something is enough to make you quit." In other words, if you keep picking something up and putting it back down in the wrong places—like catalogues, unopened mail, loose coins, or sunglasses that end up cluttering your dining table or kitchen counters—it's not because you're an abysmal organizational failure or because you were born messy! It's simply because you haven't taken the time to assign those items their own special homes. The whole notion of assigning everything its own place can actually be fun. Just imagine how happy your car keys would feel if they could take a nap in their own ceramic bowl on your kitchen counter; imagine how giddy those tennis balls would feel if they could bounce home into their own bucket in your hall closet. By assigning everything its own spot, you end up feeling so much better ... and so will all your stuff. Turns out Dorothy and Toto were absolutely right in saying, "There's no place like home."

EXERCISE

Once you've categorized from the "Sort" chapter's exercise, evaluate how many containers you'll need and what sizes work best. Start by buying containers for one small area at a time so you can see what does and doesn't work for you. Decide whether you want to see what's inside the container or not. Then make an appointment to go container shopping. Bring a friend. Think outside the box, literally. If it appeals to your aesthetics and thinking style, use bulletin boards as homes for loose papers or milk crates for files. Buy nets or laundry baskets to hold stuffed animals and toys; baskets and bowls for make-up and toiletries; colorful hooks for hanging things in closets; or large see-through plastic boxes and heavy-duty shelving for garages or basements. Above all, create "homes" that meet your unique needs, style, and personality.

File

Sheila owned a beautiful, antique secretary desk where she kept everything that needed to be filed—magazines with interesting articles, unopened mail, paid and unpaid bills, recipes, receipts, copies of documents, appliance instructions, warranty booklets, medical and insurance paperwork, and more. Every few days, she'd pick something up, look at it, not really know what to do with it or where to put it, then toss it back in the pile. Whenever she felt inspired to file, she would scoop up a batch of papers from the desk and take them upstairs to the overcrowded file cabinet in her guest room. Most of the folders were frayed and dog-eared, with scribbled, unclear headings, and she couldn't find the files she needed. (Not that she could have fit anything in them, anyway.) Frustrated, she'd end up bringing the paperwork back to the secretary desk, vowing to file it another day.

Sound familiar? If your filing system is a wreck (or simply nonexistent), don't despair. Once you understand the basic idea behind filing, the rest can be easy and even fun.

The first step is recognizing what makes a good system. "Organize your files the way you actually use them," says June Saruwatari. "A good filing system is one that everybody understands and that doesn't have to be recreated every year. And you don't have to file more than once a month if you spend the time and energy to set up a good system that works for you."

Evaluate why your current filing system isn't working for you. Is the file cabinet too crowded, inaccessible, or far away? Is your system too complex? Are the files torn up and illegible? Have you kept every piece of paper since the beginning of time? If it would help you evaluate more clearly, make a list of everything you don't like about your filing system—or talk it out with a friend.

Once you get a sense of what's not working, it's time to decide which filing system feels best: a traditional system, based on filing in alphabetical order or by subject matter; or a numerical system, such as those used by larger organizations like libraries and medical centers. Barry Izsak of the National Association of Professional Organizers, loves the Paper Tiger numerical filing system (www.papertiger.com). He explains that this software program is like, "an Internet search engine for your files, like Googling for your file cabinet." The program serves as a master index of your numbered files with a descriptive list of what's inside each file (which you decide). No need to fret about categorizing or alphabetizing—you can have two hundred or two thousand files if you like. When you search for something, you simply type some key words— such as, "love letter from high school sweetheart"—and the software instantly tells you it's hiding in file number seven.

You don't have to remember where anything goes because the computerized index remembers. Fans of this system swear by it. (You can, of course, create a noncomputerized numerical filing system by numbering your files and writing your own master index with a description of what's in each file.)

But if tigers and numbers make you sweat, no worries. Alphabets and subjects work—just follow these basic principles. Choose a few broad categories, says June Saruwatari, like Money, Household, Medical, and Career—too many categories can become confusing. Within each category, create subcategories and organize them in alphabetical order (for instance, put Bank Statements, Investments, and Tax Info into the Money category). Use either hanging or expandable files; get sturdy file folders that don't sag or slip inside the main file; and always label everything very clearly (using big block letters, a label from a label maker, or labels printed from your computer). If you decide to group files by subject, you can have fun with colors, grouping the financial files in green, household in pink, and so on; this can make them more aesthetically pleasing, while also helping you spot files quickly and easily.

What to do with all that paper that keeps flowing into your life, once you've filed your existing papers? Create an in-box (which could be a basket or file tray). What goes in that in-box? According to Saruwatari, "Everything that needs to be reviewed, sorted, and decided upon." She recommends waiting to go through your mail "until you're ready to sit down and file it or put it in its proper place." And when you know something is ready to be filed, either file it then or there, or put it in a "to file" tray; every month (or whenever the tray gets full) set a timer and take ten or twenty minutes to slip those papers into existing files. She also suggests creating an "action" file or box to hold paperwork that must be acted on very soon, i.e., bills and important letters.

What exactly needs to be filed away? Ultimately that's a personal decision. Obviously you want to file papers related to legal and tax issues. We also file papers that have personal significance, like our child's completed homework, letters from old friends, current instruction manuals, decorating ideas, and so on. Instead of saving magazines to read later, tear out the articles you're interested in and file them in a folder that you check (and purge) every month. Pay attention to what does not need to be filed—old paid bills, drafts of completed projects, duplicates and triplicates of papers, manuals from equipment long gone, ancient hospital correspondence, expired memberships, and so on. When it doubt, toss it out! Ask yourself, what's the worst thing that can happen if I throw it away?

If paper does start piling up and you're feeling stressed, remember what author Lee Silber says: There aren't any paper police waiting to arrest us for not filing. And filing happens to be a left-brain function. That's why many creative, right-brain folks prefer having their stuff where they can see it, says Silber. They love his "Pile, Don't File" system. Neaten up the piles on your desk, he says, "Then wrap a large piece of paper around each grouping to create a spine. . . . Label each area of your pile and with a quick glance get a clue as to what's in the stack." You can even divide your desk into quadrants, he adds, and place papers appropriately.

Evaluate your filing system. Does it work for you? Start by purging five older files that you'll never need to access again. Throw out duplicates, ancient receipts, and so on. Replace ragged folders with new ones and label them clearly. Don't have a filing system? Decide which type feels intuitively right and set it up. Finally, create an action center, including an in-box, a "take action" tray, and a "to file" tray.

Recycle

J ackie loved recycling. In addition to carting newspapers, cans, and bottles to her neighborhood recycling center, she also recycled clothes by shopping at thrift stores and rummage sales and then donating clothes back to those organizations. Once, at a church rummage sale, she hit the jackpot with a Neiman Marcus dress that still had the original price tag on it: $1,600. She paid only five dollars for it! But nearly a year later, while she was decluttering her closet, she discovered that dress stuck in the back. She had never worn it because it never fit comfortably. When her daughter's school announced their annual fundraiser auction, Jackie decided to donate that Neiman Marcus dress. To her delight, it sold for $675. "Not only does recycling help the earth," she told friends, "but it can end up supporting schools, too!"

Consider this statistic from the National Association of Professional Organizers: We wear 20 percent of the clothes we own only 80 percent of the time—the rest hangs there just in case. So why not recycle some of those unused items by passing them on to someone who can really enjoy them? If it's too much of a bother to recycle clothes, furniture, paper, plastic, cans, and glass, ponder the disturbing fact that the waste generated by the United States would actually fill a convoy of ten-ton garbage trucks lined up halfway to the moon. Recycling whenever we can, whether it's carrying newspapers to the recycling center or donating clothes and household items to charities, is an easy, wonderful way to feel good, help others, support the environment, and keep your space clutter free.

There are literally hundreds of organizations, church groups, shelters, and charities that would leap at the chance to lighten your load. If donating clothes is something you enjoy doing, then make an actual space for donations in your house. "If your intention is to truly recycle," says June Saruwatari, "and you love the whole notion of giving and receiving, then create a permanent bin in your closet called "give-away." Creating the physical space sets the intention into action." This way, each time you encounter an item that you no longer use or need, you can put it right into the bin and then, once a week or once a month, give it all away.

It's easy to donate books and magazines to libraries, schools, hospitals, and nursing homes. Many charities such as Big Brothers, Big Sisters, or the National Kidney Foundation will gladly pick up items from your home and leave you a receipt (you fill in the worth of the items) that can be deducted from your taxes. Many animal shelters would be grateful for donations of old towels and sheets. Recycling anything in decent condition—whether it's household goods, dishes, knickknacks, clothes, shoes, toys, tools, small furniture or appliances—is a great way to keep your home constantly fresh and orderly.

Buying and selling used items on sites like www.craigslist.com is another form of recycling. For families, another great idea is joining a toy cooperative, which is basically a toy library. Instead of adding to your kid's clutter by buying expensive new toys, you can take your child to borrow toys from the co-op each week. Parents spend less, toys get recycled, and everyone wins. If there aren't any co-ops in your areas, start your own. Many churches or community centers are willing to donate a room where you can keep the toys. The co-op idea could work for books, CDs, DVDs, and magazines as well. Gather a bunch of friends, put your co-op items in plastic containers, and open the co-op on certain days (manned by volunteers); this way, everyone will have neater, more spacious homes. There are also plenty of places to recycle or trade items online, such as sites like www.ReSpinIt.com, which allows the trading of used DVDs.

Recycling gifts, especially for children, is another way to keep clutter to a minimum. One child's least favorite teddy bear or train set can be another kid's newfound treasure. Check with some of the families in your social circle and see if they want to start recycling gifts with you and your children instead of buying new gifts.

You can also recycle odd objects in your house by giving them new uses, suggests Lee Silber. Vases can hold paint brushes, sentimental knickknacks can become bookends, soap dishes can hold paper clips, an interesting nonfunctional musical instrument can make a great wall decoration. If you really want to hold on to it, come up with creative ways to recycle it.

Invite three or more friends to a trading party. Have each person bring at least three items they no longer need, such as clothes, jewelry, books, housewares, and duplicate electronic equipment. Put all the items on the table. If you want, you can all just jump in and start claiming items (if two people fall in love with the same thing, play a childhood game, like Rock Paper Scissors, to decide who gets it). Or you can draw numbers to select an order, and then have one person at a time choose an item from the table. Once someone has all the things they want, they can pass when their turn comes around. Have a donate bin for any leftovers, and donate them to charity.

Clean

Don Aslett, America's top cleaning expert, thinks that we waste too much time cleaning: "We spend an average of five years of our lives on household cleaning and maintenance—that's a lot of 'life' taken out of our time on earth!" He believes that the antidote to spending enormous amounts of time cleaning is prevention. Simplify your life, reduce the clutter, buy less, and you won't need to dust and clean nearly as much.

Of course, even after you've already simplified, your home will still need some cleaning. But Aslett's first advice about cleaning is to "avoid overkill." Too much cleaning is as bad as too little. If you're spending more than a few hours each week cleaning, you're cleaning inefficiently. To get more efficient, Aslett suggests setting your own standard of cleanliness rather than figuring out a cleaning schedule. Instead of when to clean the windows, decide how clean you want them to be. Prefer windows that are smudge-free? That's a standard, explains Aslett, not a schedule. "We should clean by necessity, not schedule, habit, or appointment," he writes in his book, *No Time to Clean.* "Why mop the floor twice a week if it's still clean and shiny, or vacuum daily if there is no dirt?" When it comes to deciding when to clean, he says, "Trust what you see, feel, smell, and even hear (the complaints.)"

Equally important is buying the right cleaning tools, the kind professionals use, and getting rid of all the other stuff advertised on television and in magazines. For windows, Aslett recommends buying a professional squeegee, tossing out the whole idea of cleaning with vinegar, and using "a dollar's worth of dishwashing liquid in a bucket of water." Your windows will sparkle. Throw away your old-fashioned sponge mops and brooms. Buy the high-tech microfiber cloths. They can be used alone to clean and dust almost any surface and can also be used as mops to clean everything from grime to pet hair to scruff marks.

When it comes to dusting, Aslett writes, "Up to 80 percent of the dust and dirt that gets into a house comes in through the doors." He recommends using high-quality doormats inside and out. You can also reduce dusting, other experts agree, by vacuuming before you dust (but check the vacuum bag regularly to make sure it's not spewing particles.)

And don't forget to clear away those cobwebs hidden in corners and on light fixtures, because feng shui expert Katherine Thurston says doing so will help clear your past as well.

Another strategy that can help with the deeper, more thorough cleaning is to take on one room each month. This way you get to really focus on every aspect of that room. Make a list of all the things you can do to that particular room when the month arrives—things you wouldn't normally do on a daily basis, like flipping mattresses in bedrooms; replacing batteries and light bulbs in the living room; wiping down walls, telephone receivers, and computer screens in the office; laundering plastic shower liners; polishing silverware in the dining room and so on. And treat each room to a wonderful fragrance by adding twenty droplets of your favorite essential oil to a spray bottle. Just mist and say ahhhh . . .

Of course, sometimes this one-room-a-month system might need to be adjusted if disaster strikes. Aslett firmly believes in cleaning on the spot, whenever things get dirty, because it saves you time and energy later on. "Become more conscious," he writes. "So much of the mess making we do each day is a matter of simple oblivion." Knocking over that coffee cup, walking in with muddy shoes, dropping potato chips on the carpet—these are the kinds of behaviors that cause us more work down the road. "Cleaning can be reduced more by behavior change than anything else," Aslett says. "What doesn't get dirtied or abused doesn't require care!"

EXERCISE

Create a "cleaning center" for your home. Declutter, clean, and pretty-up the mess under your kitchen sink (or pick your messiest supply closet.) Throw away all the old unnecessary cleaning supplies, replenish what's needed, put down new contact paper, or paint the area with a bright, fun color. Organize items with wire baskets, colorful plastic boxes, or interesting hooks that can hold your cleaning tools and appliances. Then decide how clean you need things to be, pick a room in your house, gather everyone in your household, and spend a couple of hours doing your deep cleaning for the month.

Schedule

Effortlessly Managing the Flow of Time

"An unhurried sense of time is in itself a form of wealth."
—BONNIE FRIEDMAN

Organizing your day is not all that different from organizing your closet. In fact, time management expert Julie Morgenstern writes in her bestseller *Time Management from the Inside Out,* "Just as a closet is a limited space into which you must fit a certain number of objects, a schedule is a limited space into which you must fit a limited number of tasks. Your days are not infinite and endless. When you think of it this way, time is not so intangible and elusive. In fact, each day is simply a container, a storage unit that has a definite capacity you can reach." So grab your watch, because it's time now for us to get curious (and brave) about meeting that frantic white rabbit that lives within us all-you know, the one with the giant pocket watch who hops around shouting, "I'm late, I'm late, for a very important date!" With the strategies and advice from our experts, we'll have our inner white rabbits arriving happily on time after all!

Value

A my was a busy mother and part-time bookkeeper. When she was single, she loved spending time in museums and taking yoga classes. But ever since she became a mother, those things seem to drift away. Every New Year's Eve she promised herself she'd sign up for a class that inspired her. But whenever her kids or husband wanted something or her employer needed something, Amy felt obliged to give every ounce of herself. One afternoon, after working extra hours at the office, she raced off to pick up the kids at school because her husband had promised a colleague he'd play a round of golf. She drove the kids to soccer practice, then got home late and frantically made dinner. By the time her husband walked in at 7:00 p.m., Amy snapped. "I never get to do what I want!" Bursting into tears, she stormed upstairs and slammed the bedroom door, feeling angry and deeply unappreciated. She spent a long time thinking about what really mattered to her in life. Family was important, to be sure, but she also deeply valued her creative spirit and spiritual side. Yet whenever she had the chance to sign up for classes, she would talk herself out of it. Then and there, she began writing a mission statement for herself—something that reflected who she really was and what really mattered to her. Now it would be easier, she thought, to evaluate and make decisions about all the choices that life presented.

Whether you're having a good day or a bad day, one thing remains constant: With only 168 hours in every week, your time is limited. And how you spend those fleeting seconds (86,400 in a day) greatly impacts the quality of your inner and outer life. As time management expert Harold Taylor points out, "We cannot manage time. Nor can we save it. Time ticks away relentlessly in spite of our efforts to control it. We can use it wisely or we can waste it."

Barry Izsak sums it up this way: "Time management is about self-management." And self-management, these experts agree, begins with defining your own unique values. "Values underlie what's truly important to us," says life coach Natalie Gahrmann, author of *Succeeding as a Super Busy Parent.* "When you become really clear about what's important to you, you can live your life consciously based on that. Because life is so busy, we don't really take the time to reflect on what's really and truly most important to us."

The first step in navigating through our stormy or calm 168-hour week is understanding what makes us tick, what drives our life, what's most important to us. "When you're clear on your values," says Gahrmann, "they serve as a guide-post in your decision making." The essence of effective time management is about making the best decisions you can, every single day, based on your deepest values.

In addition to clarifying our values, we also need to value our own time. Too many of us live our lives like Amy, ignoring what's important, and disrespecting our time. "By valuing your time," says Gahrmann, "you're valuing yourself. If you don't value your time, nobody else will." How do you know if you're valuing your time? "You feel respected and appreciated," says Gahrmann. "You don't feel resentful of other people and you don't feel taken advantage of."

Gahrmann believes that it's equally important to value others' time. "When someone says "enough," we need to respect that. The problem is that we don't. We keep pushing and cajoling and trying to persuade them, because we ourselves are so overwhelmed."

Since we don't have infinite hours and we want to live the best life we can, we need to take some of that precious time to genuinely respect ourselves—and offer that same respect to others. And we need to recognize what underlying values drive us. Once we begin to do that, we can more easily make decisions that reflect those core values. If writing a novel is really important to you, then the next time you have to choose between an all-day party at the house of someone you barely know or staying home to rewrite a chapter, you'll make a wiser choice based on your deepest desire.

Contemplate the quality of how you spend your time. Do you ever feel angry or resentful? If so, that's a clue that perhaps you're undervaluing yourself and your time. In order to get clearer on your values around time, make two lists: "The top ten things I really want to do" (focusing especially on things you rarely or never do that you would enjoy). And "The top ten things I don't want to do that I do too much." Once you have a list of what you'd like to do more often, schedule fifteen to thirty minutes every day this week to enjoy one of these activities. It could be as simple as sitting in a garden, reading a chapter of a novel, painting your toenails, or playing the guitar. Also this week, play with writing a personal mission statement based on your values. It can be as simple as "I want to live a life filled with adventure and excitement," or "I want to be peaceful, surrounded by the people and things that I love." Your mission statement, which can continually change or expand, simply acts as a lighthouse, guiding you closer to your heartfelt desires.

Prioritize

Thomas, a time management expert who loved giving presentations at conferences once delivered his message to a group of business people in a unique way. He placed a big jar on a table in front of the audience. Then he took out a bag of large rocks. One by one, he put the large rocks into the jar until the jar was filled up. "Is it full?" he asked his audience. They all shouted, "Yes." He then pulled out a bag of gravel and dumped it in the jar. "Is it full now?" he asked again. The audience shouted, "Yes" for a second time. Smiling, he hauled out a bucket of fine sand and began pouring it into the jar, filling up all the empty spaces. "How about now?" he asked, "Is it full?" By now the audience caught on. "No!" they shouted back. He pulled out a glass pitcher of water and slowly emptied it into the jar. When he was done, he asked, "What's the point of all this? What's the message?" A young executive eagerly replied, "We can always fit more things into our schedules no matter how busy we are!" The audience laughed, nodding in agreement, but Thomas shook his head.

"No," he said, lifting the jar packed with rocks, gravel, sand, and water. "The point to all this is that if you don't put the big rocks in first, you'll never fit them in at all."

Barry Izsak wholeheartedly agrees. "Every time you do something unimportant," he says, "you are trading something important for it." Prioritizing means looking at the "big rocks" and making time and space for them in our busy day.

"We cannot do every thing," reminds Harold Taylor. "It is a life of choices. We must choose those activities that will have the greatest positive impact on our life.... Set goals for your personal life as well as your business or work and the priorities will become obvious."

If you're not sure if something is a priority or not, Taylor has the following suggestion: "Ask yourself what the result would be if you failed to do it. If the consequence would be negligible, it's probably not a priority. If it would do nothing to further a goal, it's probably not a priority."

Author Lee Silber says, "The most important time management tool is a to-do list." Many time management experts suggest using a to-do list and a master list concurrently. The master list is the overview and serves as a guide. You create it based on your values and goals, and put in everything you want to accomplish in all the areas of your life—career, finances, relationships, self-care, travel, and so on. Creating a master list first can help ensure that your daily to-do lists are helping you get closer to your larger life goals.

To make an effective to-do list, remember not to fill it with a hundred tasks that can't be accomplished in a day. Silber explains that "People make long lists that are impossible to do in one day. When they don't get it done, they feel terrible about themselves." He suggests using your master list to help you create a daily to-do list, by breaking down your overarching goals into what he calls "micro-movements: small incremental easy simple daily things to get you there." This way you always have a sense of moving forward, especially if you take on at least one difficult task every day.

If there's a large and difficult task that you want to accomplish, some experts suggest using the "Swiss cheese method," in which you poke holes in the task by doing small pieces of it in any order. This helps you enjoy the task and can head off procrastination and feelings of being overwhelmed.

If you're a right-brained sort, Silber suggests that your to-do list doesn't have to be in a linear form. "It can be three piles left on a desk—that's the same as writing it down on a list. It can be doodles or a stack of post-its." As you make your to-do list for the day, allow yourself to find the method that intuitively works for you.

EXERCISE

Take some time this week to create your master list. List all of your "big rocks"—the ultimate goals in all the major areas of your life. Then take these goals, break them down into small doable steps, and set a realistic time frame for completing each step. Pick a target date for each of your smaller goals. Each day, before making your daily to-do list, briefly scan this master list and allow it to inform your priorities for the day. Once you have your short daily to-do list, rank each activity in order of importance.

Plan

Before I began writing this book, I actually used three different calendars: a large one on the wall in my kitchen by the phone so I could schedule things when people called; another one in my home office; and a third purse-sized daily planner I carried with me almost every day. One morning I realized I was in trouble when the birthday party my son had been invited to (scribbled on the kitchen calendar) ended up being on the same afternoon as both a dentist's appointment (scheduled in my portable calendar) and a phone meeting (scrawled on my office calendar). Yikes! I knew I needed a better system to manage my busy life.

Every expert I interviewed for this book agreed that when it comes to sophisticated calendar systems and daily planners, a single calendar or daily planner for both business and personal life is the best strategy. "Simple is better," insists Barry Izsak. "People think getting vast and complicated systems is better, but they won't stick to them because they're too complex." Life coach Natalie Gahrmann concurs that "Multiple calendars means multiple chaos."

Many of us think that if only we could find the perfect planner, we'd achieve perfect organization. Yet time management expert Harold Taylor points out that it isn't the planner; it's the way you use it: "People are not organized because they use a time management system," says Taylor. "They use a time management system because they are organized."

The last chapter discussed the importance of to-do lists, yet Izsak and Taylor insist that in order to make to-do lists work, you must actually schedule the specific tasks in your calendar. "A to-do list is simply a wish list," says Izsak. "It's not a commitment until you schedule time in your planner to actually accomplish the tasks. . . . A calendar system is only as good as its user. The best system in the world is not going to last if you don't stick to it. Create a system that works for you."

Once you've settled on a single calendar, Taylor says, "Schedule appointments with yourself to get the priority work done. Once you actually schedule time, resist any temptation to use this time for less important spur-of-the-moment things. Pretend they are appointments with your surgeon. . . . Block out distractions and concentrate on the task at hand." When the scheduled time comes to clean your closet, work on that novel, or spend time with your loved ones, turn off your phone's ringer, turn off your e-mail, and focus.

Another key in actually implementing your plan is making sure you don't overschedule yourself. Otherwise, says Taylor, "you'll be constantly rescheduling tasks and putting yourself under pressure. Leave space in your planner to handle those unforeseen emergencies and additional priorities that pop up." He recommends scheduling "no more than 50 percent of your time." Izsak adds that one way to save time is to avoid, "spending inordinate amounts of time on a task that doesn't warrant it or require it, like five hours to organize your refrigerator." So spend an hour to clean out the fridge, and once that hour is over, let the rest of it go, even if it's not picture perfect.

Effectively planning and implementing your day also includes knowing when you're the most energetic. Are you a morning or afternoon person? What time of day works best for you? What time of day holds more distractions for you? Do your kids come home in the afternoon? Then don't schedule tasks in the afternoon that need your intense focus or concentration. Schedule your most challenging tasks when you're the most alert and focused. "Clump all your appointments and meetings together," adds Izsak. "Don't break up the day with an 8:00 a.m. meeting and a 2:00 p.m. meeting. You need a big span of time to get work done." Always schedule two hours at a time for important tasks-blocks of uninterrupted time during which you don't answer calls or e-mails.

And for those right-brainers out there, Lee Silber would like to remind you that your plan for the day "doesn't have to be linear." If using a day planner or calendar feels overwhelming or confusing, Silber suggests alternatives: "You can create a visual map, with a drawing showing all the different places you have to go that day."

Sometimes the best-laid plans must be changed because of unforeseen events. But that doesn't mean that having a plan in the first place isn't useful. In the end, says Izsak, "Plans are the handrails to guide you through your days' distractions and keep you on course. You're way better off having a plan and changing it than not having a plan at all."

EXERCISE

If you don't have a day planner, buy one (and only one!). This week, practice choosing two to three tasks every day from your prioritized to-do list and scheduling them into your calendar. Pick one particularly difficult task you've been avoiding and block uninterrupted time (ninety minutes to two hours) to work on that task.

Delegate

Six months after Brian started his own company, he was staying up late every night reading reports, doing the billing, and handling problems. From the moment he stepped into the office, he felt pressured. Although he had hired a small staff, Brian seemed to have increasingly more work. When his wife suggested he turn over some of the tasks to his staff, Brian would inevitably get angry. "They can't do it the way I do it!" When things got bad enough, he'd ask his staff to do trivial things, leaving the difficult ones for himself. "If I want this done right, I have to do it myself!" The few times he did give an employee something important, he wouldn't leave them alone, micromanaging every move. "I can't trust her," he'd think. Or he'd get too impatient trying to explain exactly how he wanted it done: "She's not qualified to do this." It was no surprise his staff constantly quit, and when they did, Brian would think, "You just can't find a good employee these days!"

The ability to delegate is crucial in managing your time productively, says Harold Taylor, author of *Making Time Work for You.* "Delegation extends results from what you can do personally to what you can control. It frees time for more important tasks, allows you to plan more effectively, and helps relieve the pressure of too many jobs, too many deadlines, and too little time."

For those of us who have a hard time delegating, it may be because, like Brian, we think we need to be in total control, or we don't trust others' abilities. Often we're convinced we're the only ones who can do the job right. For some of us, even if we want to delegate, we don't; maybe we're scared to ask for help, worried we'll be rejected, or concerned we'll be too much of a burden. Or maybe we never delegate because we simply don't know how. There are plenty of reasons why delegating can feel challenging, but once we can identify these undermining attitudes and begin delegating anyway, the benefits are enormous.

Whether you're sharing responsibility with people in your family or your office, delegating makes life easier and more fun. "One of the bonuses you receive from effective delegation," says Taylor, "is that in many cases the job is better in the hands of someone else." Someone else's fresh perspective or unique talents come into play. "But don't delegate nonproductive or unprofitable trivia. Eliminate them instead."

When you do turn a task over to someone else, really turn it over, says Taylor. "Be sure to delegate the authority as well as the responsibility. Don't continually look over their shoulder, interfere with their methods, or jump on them when they make mistakes. Make sure you're delegating the objective, not the actual procedure. And be prepared to trade short-term errors for long-term results."

One of those unexpected long-term results can be building someone else's self-esteem. "Don't always delegate to the most capable people," Taylor suggests. "Delegation is one of the most effective methods of developing others."

EXERCISE

Make a list of ten tasks in your busy life that could be delegated to someone else—from hiring a babysitter or housekeeper to inviting a friend to share your volunteering work. Then make a list of ten tasks you don't want to delegate because you think no one can do them as well as you. Circle two tasks from each list, brainstorm who might be a great person to delegate to (or who might really benefit from doing the task), and then delegate. Experiment! See how it feels to delegate some of the tasks on your second list. Remember, this is an exercise in letting go and also an opportunity to be supported, once again, by sharing your responsibilities.

Assert

J udy always took care of everyone. Whenever a new committee formed at the PTA, they always asked Judy to join
it. Flattered by their faith in her and wanting to be helpful,
she always said yes. If a neighbor needed help, she was there.
Everyone felt comfortable asking Judy to do things. When she
began having severe stomach pains, she immediately scheduled an appointment with her doctor. After a few tests, they
discovered she had the beginnings of an ulcer. Realizing how
stress was impacting her, Judy starting seeing a therapist, who
suggested that perhaps she needed to say "no" more of the
time. The idea of refusing anyone anything terrified Judy at
first—what if people got mad at her or thought she didn't
care? But with her therapist's support, she began to politely
but firmly turn down invitations and requests. Much to her
surprise, she began feeling freer and happier—and her stomach problems cleared up.

Dr. Robert Sapolsky writes in his book *Why Zebras Don't
Get Ulcers,* "Mammals don't get ulcers because they do not

normally harbor chronic stress. That is something we humans do all the time." So much of our stress comes from taking on too much, or taking on things that don't ultimately serve our greatest good. The stress of overcommitting ourselves and chronically doing too much can contribute to an entire host of problems, ranging from ulcers to depression to complete burnout. Mark Gorkin, The Stress Doc™, sums it up succinctly: "A firm 'no' a day keeps the ulcers away."

The ability (and willingness) to assert ourselves and say "no" is fundamental, experts agree, in managing ourselves and our time effectively. It all comes down to choice, insists Harold Taylor: "We seem to be unaware that saying yes to something that will demand a lot of our time is the same as saying no to something else—whether it's reading a book, spending a few hours with the family, or going for a walk. It's more than just a decision to say yes or no—it's a choice we make as to how we will spend our time."

Why is it so difficult to say "no"? We may be afraid of hurting or disappointing people. Perhaps we're scared of what we perceive as our own aggressiveness. Sometimes we think that saying "no" to someone might come off as being too arrogant or superior. Or maybe saying "no" brings up feelings of inadequacy, because it reminds us that we can't personally be everything to everyone. We all have our healthy limits, but sometimes it can be hard to remember that those limits aren't failures.

Life coach Marilyn Nagel says that saying "no" can actually be easier than we think. We don't have to be aggressive in order to be assertive. Remember, says Nagel, that what ultimately matters most is your relationship with the person, not whether you fulfill their request. She suggests a four-step process in saying no:

1. Acknowledge the person for who they are in your life. (If Judy was asked to join another PTA Committee, she might tell the person how much she enjoyed working with them in the past and how easy they were to collaborate with.)
2. Thank them for thinking of you to do this. (She'd then genuinely thank them for asking her to participate again.)
3. Acknowledge the quality of what they are offering you. (Next, she'd let them know how important that committee is and how much it could help the school.)
4. Suggest an alternative solution. (Finally, she'd mention asking Alberta, the new parent who had just joined the PTA, because Alberta specialized in what that committee was all about.)

Remember that if you initially say "yes," you can always change your mind, says psychotherapist Cindy Glovinsky: "It's okay to go back and say no." Don't feel like you need some elaborate excuse; all you need to offer is a simple "no thank you" without any added explanation. If someone keeps pressuring you, simply (but firmly) keep saying "no."

Take the time to notice how you're feeling when someone makes a request. Postpone giving an answer immediately so you can carefully evaluate each request. Are you already over-committed? Do you feel stressed? When planning your daily life, never ignore your health and well-being—otherwise everyone ends up losing.

If saying "no" is hard for you, try the following visualizing exercise. First, imagine a scenario in which you'd like to be more assertive. Imagine that you're being asked to do something you don't want to do, and give yourself a chance to picture this situation in your mind's eye. Hear yourself saying "yes" to this request, and tune in to how your body feels when you agree to something you don't want to do. Does your chest feel tight or does your stomach feel tense? Do you feel sad or scared or angry? Allow yourself to observe the scene in full detail, experiencing viscerally how it feels to say "yes" when you mean "no." Breathe through the uncomfortable feelings. Then open your eyes, take some deep breaths, and shake off this experience. Now imagine the same request being made, but this time imagine using the four-step process to say "no." Be conscious of how this feels in your body—you may feel lighter, looser, or more energized by speaking your truth. Now, commit to trying out this four-step process of saying "no" at least once this week.

Monitor

Patricia worked at home as a freelance graphic artist, but having her office in her little apartment could be tremendously distracting. For instance, whenever she went online to check e-mail she'd end up spending an hour following links people sent and surfing the Web. Or when her friend Sara called, Patricia ended up talking for more than an hour. By the end of the day, she never felt like she'd accomplished enough. One day, while using an electronic timer to bake cookies, it occurred to Patricia that she could use this same timer in other areas of her life. The next time Sara called, Patricia set the timer for twenty minutes. When it quietly beeped, she politely told Sara she had to go. Soon Patricia began using the timer everywhere. She'd set it for twenty minutes to do the accounting work she hated; twenty minutes for cleaning the bathroom; twenty minutes to declutter her desk; twenty minutes to check e-mail. Even meditating, which she always wanted to do but resisted, became easier when she set a timer for twenty minutes. "A timer is a wonderful way to keep me on track," she says. "And it's a powerful tool against procrastination because I'm willing to do almost anything for twenty minutes. It really helps me develop new habits—and let go of ones that don't serve me anymore."

If you truly want to live your life in ways that support your broadest goals and desires, then becoming aware of how you spend your time can be invaluable. If daily habits like watching television, talking on the phone, or reading e-mail are robbing you of hours that you wish were better spent, a timer can be a simple and easy way to keep your day in check. Computer consultant Karen Simon, suggests, "Place the timer in another room, so you don't hit the snooze button to keep working." This way you'll have to get up out of your chair to shut it off. This can break the obsessive energy that Simon says many of us experience when we're surfing the Internet or playing computer games.

"Keeping a time log can also be a great awareness-building tool," says life coach Natalie Gahrmann. "You can set your watch or cell phone to go off every thirty minutes and then jot down what you're doing right then and there. It's a way to keep track." Of course, that might drive some of us crazy, adds Gahrmann. "So you can also just pause right before you do something new and ask yourself, 'Is this something really important to me? Will this pull me closer to my goal or push me further away? Will this contribute to who I am and what's important?'"

According to Lee Silber, "The right side of the brain has no clock in it and no concept of time." All of us have experienced that sense of timelessness when we're engaged in an activity we love, but right-brainers can regularly get lost in a timeless space. If this is the case for you, Silber suggests putting an extra-large clock in your office to remind you of the time.

If you constantly underestimate how long things take, monitoring your time can be a great support. Every time management expert I spoke to agreed that we need to overestimate how long things take in general. If you believe traveling from the mall to the meeting takes thirty minutes, overestimate and assume it will take sixty minutes. If you arrive ahead of time, great! You'll feel relaxed instead of rushed. And you can use the extra minutes to make calls or read a magazine. This way you'll always feel ahead, instead of ever-behind.

EXERCISE

For half the week, keep an activity log without changing what you normally do. Jot down what you do, what time of day you do it, and about how long you spend doing it. Also record how you feel at that time of day (for instance, tired, alert, frustrated, relaxed, productive, sleepy, and so on). The second half of the week, play this game: Use a timer or alarm and actually time how long activities take to complete. If you think it's going to take forty minutes to get across town after the meeting, time it to see if you're right. Do you think you spend twenty minutes checking your e-mails? Time it and see how long you really sit at the computer. Notice if you tend to under-estimate. With this new awareness, you can then begin overestimating—and see how much fun it is to arrive right on time!

Compute

My husband, Dennis, owns a maintenance and repair business. Every week he drives hundreds of miles servicing residential and commercial clients. During the day, his truck is his office. For years he wrote people's names and addresses on crumpled scraps of paper, kept important notes on the backs of receipts, and scribbled appointments on fast-food containers. When it came time to bill customers, Dennis would often forget to update their invoice after a repair. He knew he was losing money and time.

When a friend who specialized in electronic organizers suggested he buy a hand-held computer, Dennis purchased a Palm Pilot. In a matter of weeks, his entire business transformed. Now he has a pocket-sized computer which contains every appointment and all the contact information for his customers and vendors. When he gets back into his truck after a complicated repair, he inputs his hours and the services they involved. After he gets home, he connects the Palm to his computer and uploads the updated information, so that if he loses the Palm all the information will be saved. That little gadget completely changed his work life.

According to the U.S. Department of Commerce, more than 66 percent of the population use computers. Yet despite the millions of Americans sitting in front of computer screens every day, too many still don't realize how computers can save them time.

Computerizing specific areas of your personal and business life can save huge amounts of time, money, and energy, says Karen Simon, owner of PC Tech Associates, a small business computer consulting firm. She says the first step is recognizing what the computer really is: "It's a place to put things. Just like you have a closet for linens and a drawer for eyeglasses, you have to have a central place for your information." A computer is where you dump all the details of your life. "If you clutter your home, it makes you feel uncomfortable and stressed. Why clutter your brain?"

There are several areas of your life that can be made more efficient by computerizing. Here are the ones Simon recommends:

Finances: Save time and energy by setting up online bill paying (or software to print out checks) and using programs that track expenses, tax information, and investments.

Address book: Input all your contact information (along with specific notes helping you remember any details about personal and business contacts) and then recycle the paper clutter.

Appointments: Computers have easy calendar programs, too, so you can use a computer instead of a paper calendar or day planner to keep track of important appointments and even be reminded when they're coming up. (If you already have a daily planner or calendar set up, you can play with the computer to see if you'd ultimately prefer computerizing your appointments.)

Research. Using the Internet for researching information about every subject under the sun saves untold hours normally spent in a library. Simon suggests that you toss out dusty dictionaries and heavy phone books, because all that information is easily available online.

Another way to save time is to organize the computer itself more efficiently, says Simon. "A computer is a cubbyhole to store pieces of information. Just like the cubbyholes from kindergarten which had each child's name, you want to separate or categorize each piece of information by topic or type of item." Instead of having hundreds of e-mail files, Simon recommends categorizing them into folders the way you would paper files. Do the same with your documents.

Consider buying a hand-held electronic organizer such as a Blackberry or Palm Pilot. From Simon's point of view, it's an invaluable investment. "If you lost your (paper) daily planner, you'd lose everything," she says. But once those names and addresses are computerized and backed up on your personal computer, they're safe, organized, and easy to update. In addition to containing all your appointments and contact information, these minicomputers can store to-do lists and notes.

Be sure to back up data from your computer on a routine basis, Simon emphasizes. Whether you're backing up onto CDs, DVDs, or an external hard drive, taking the time to do so (or hiring someone else to do it for you) will save you life-times of stress if your computer ever crashes.

EXERCISE

Pick an area of your daily life that can be computerized, whether on your personal computer or on a hand-held device. Schedule an appointment with yourself and take steps to streamline this area of your life. For example, you may want to start by creating a comprehensive electronic address book. As you input information, categorize the names by profession (doctor, lawyer, repairmen) or by relationship to you (close friends, neighbors, cousins). Once you're done, make sure to back up your work, and then give yourself a reward for taking this ultimately time-saving step.

Unplug

Sheila sat on the beach in Maui feeling gloriously peaceful. Minutes later she was jarred out of her reverie by a loud voice. "What do you mean the client pulled out?!" A few feet away, an attractive man paced back and forth in the sand, barking into a cell phone, a laptop open on his beach blanket. "Call Terry right now!" the man shouted, oblivious to Sheila's gaze. "Tell him to fix this!" Disgusted, the man threw his cell phone on the blanket. Then he sat down and began furiously typing on the laptop. Every few seconds, he'd check his Palm Pilot. Sheila couldn't believe it when his beeper went off. Then a pretty woman approached him, obviously his wife or girlfriend. "Let's go for a swim," she said innocently. The man glared up at her. "Are you nuts? I don't have the time..."

In 1997, Drs. Michelle Weil and Larry Rosen coined the term "technostress," describing it in their groundbreaking book, *Technostress: Coping with Technology @home @work @play:* "Because technology lets us do so much, we take on too much and end up feeling overwhelmed and never finished. We feel invaded by technology on all fronts, by the beeps of our pagers, cell phones, incoming faxes and those of others around us. We tote our laptops on vacation and our bosses expect us to carry pagers. Our personal and work boundaries are blurred and we never feel true 'down time' any more *sic*."

Technostress has led to a new kind of disorder that contemporary sociologists call "job spill." In other words, because of technology we've lost the ability to separate work from play—and it's taking its toll.

While we can't ignore the fact that technology has made our lives easier in many ways, and at times has actually saved human lives, it can also insidiously rob us of the most basic of human needs: the need to be connected, in real time, with a real, not virtual, world. "Technology promotes the idea of connection, but delivers separation," says Dr. Douglas Gerwin, a professor of child development. This separation from our essential selves, from others, and from our natural world has a negative impact on the overall quality of our lives.

"The computer is not living," computer consultant Karen Simon reminds us. What matters most, she emphasizes, "are our relationships with people." She urges us to spend more time in the real world and not sacrifice our connection to life and people for our connection to the Internet.

Experts point out that being constantly plugged in actually contributes to our sense of pressure, making us feel more harried, more rushed, and more stressed. "When you're plugged in 24/7," says life coach Jennifer Louden, "you lose the ability to have connection with your inner knowing. When you're plugged in all the time, everything is equally important, everything is fast. If you have time unplugged to slow your body down and engage with your heart, you can say, I'm human, I can only do so much."

Unplugging for periods of time can help you discover how technology truly affects your life. If you normally carry your cell phone everywhere, leave it behind this week when you run simple errands. Or shut it off and only check for emergency messages a few times a day. Also, keep a very brief techno-diary for a few days. Don't change any behaviors, just describe how interacting with technology—television, computers, cell phones, pagers, fax machines—makes you feel. Better, worse, more stressed? Like you have more time, less time? Is it easier or harder to relate to people when you're plugged in? If you see any ways that technology is negatively impacting your life, set some clear boundaries and stick to them. For example, only check e-mail and use the Internet once in the morning and once at the end of the day, for a predetermined amount of time. Determine how much TV, radio, computer, and phone interference you want in your day. And for the rest of the time, allow yourself to unplug and enjoy life.

Flow

Working with the Natural Order of the Universe

Claire always seemed to have magical days. If she was running late for an important meeting and taxis were passing her by, she'd just smile, knowing that somehow things would work out perfectly. Then she'd get a wonderful cab driver who made her laugh, and arrive at her office building at the exact same time her VIP client arrived. They'd end up chatting like old friends in the elevator and the meeting would be a grand success. Or if her washing machine broke down, she'd bump into an old friend that day at the supermarket who just happened to have the name of a fantastic repairman. Even when she was doing research on the Internet, she'd follow her instinct from one link to the next, and in no time find the exact information she needed. Friends marveled at this amazing ability. "How do you do it?" they'd always ask. Claire would smile. "I'm just in the flow."

According to Dr. Charlene Belitz, author of *The Power of Flow,* these types of magical experiences are actually a natural part of life. "Flow is a state of being where people, events, and interactions happen without our investment of time and energy." Synchronicity, says Belitz, which many might overlook as mere coincidence, comes as a result of being in flow. "I used to work in human resources," says Belitz. "I'd be sitting at my desk in a state of flow, preparing for a meeting, when it occurred to me that I needed a specific piece of information. Seconds later a colleague would show up carrying that very data." The secret, she says, is in your attitude. "When you're in flow, you look at things as perfection, without judging. Everything that happens is a gift. There are no mistakes because things happen when they're supposed to."

Belitz explains that whenever you're struggling or trying to force something that's not working and hitting lots of negativity, you're not in flow. Being in flow is always positive and delivers down-to-earth benefits. "When we let go of our pictures, ideas, and agenda about how it's supposed to look, and allow life to unfold, we have much more energy and much more time."

In case you're thinking that flow is some airy-fairy idea, Belitz is quick to explain that it's actually based on the scientific concept called Chaos Theory, which says, "There is order in the universe." She explains that our job is to just get out of the way. That's when coincidences happen. These synchronicities "are a signal that chaos has order."

What do you do when you're not in flow? Reevaluate your expectations, says Belitz. Ask two questions: Is this event or interaction really supposed to happen? Is there a truth I'm not admitting? For instance, if a meeting is not coming together easily, perhaps the timing is wrong or you secretly don't want to be involved. The more we cultivate a nonjudgmental attitude toward the events and people in our lives, the more we're in flow.

Here are five simple ways Belitz suggests you can increase flow and synchronicity:

1. Notice the meaningful coincidences/synchronicities in your life. "Increase your awareness. Enjoying the synchronicities brings peace and harmony to our lives. They give you positive feedback and let you know you're on the right track."

2. View people and events as gifts and look for the positive outcome. "Everything has a positive outcome. You have to trust it's there."

3. Take care of yourself. "View yourself as a gift," Belitz emphasizes. Rest, eat well, take vacations. "If you're not healthy and relaxed, it's harder to be in a state of flow."

4. Be in the moment. Practice mindfulness. Breathe deeply. Experience your physical senses fully so you're not trapped in your mind.

5. Serve others. "When you do, you become part of the natural rhythm of the universe. It can be as simple as a compliment or a smile. Find opportunities to serve others."

EXERCISE

This week, record all coincidences or synchronicities. Take the time to savor them. If you're in the middle of any stressful circumstance this week, consciously ask yourself: Where is the hidden gift in this? Look back at negative experiences and ponder: What is the positive outcome that I couldn't see before? For example, if you're late for a meeting because you overbooked yourself, instead of feeling bad about your mismanagement of time, practice the principles of flow. Become more present as you're hailing the taxi cab. Gently remind yourself that there's a gift in being late, even if you can't see it. Watch for any pleasant coincidences that occur the rest of the day. If you're working at your desk and are continually interrupted during an important task, instead of getting upset, cultivate the attitude that these interruptions are part of the flow, hidden gifts that you can't quite see yet. Practice the perspective that there will be a positive outcome in the situation, even if you can't imagine it at the moment.

Maintain

Staying Organized for the Rest of Your Life

"Without discipline there is no life at all."
—KATHERINE HEPBURN

You've made it to the home stretch. Your house, your office, your calendar, and your life are on the way to becoming greater sources of peacefulness, nourishment, and simplicity. Hooray! Give yourself a great big reward. Now it's time to take on this last section about the art of maintenance, which, in many ways, is the key to getting organized. If you don't keep practicing and implementing all that you've learned, these new habits, approaches, and perspectives simply won't stick. While maintenance is key to your success, it's also, thankfully, the easy part. You've already set up the systems, and now your ongoing job is to keep them fresh and flowing. Just contemplate the principles and follow the easy steps presented in this section, and you'll continue your winning streak for the rest of your life.

Practice

Cultivating Habits That Serve You

Carrie loved the new organizational book she was reading. She read through it chapter by chapter and did all the suggested exercises. In just a few weeks, her house became more ordered. Closets looked great, her garage and attic were in better shape than ever, and she was managing her time well, too. She bought copies of the book for all her friends. But then, as the months went by, things started going downhill. Her closets began getting messy again. The garage started looking terrible. Her pantry became chaotic again. And she got really, really angry. "What happened?" she wrote in a letter to the author. "I did what you said but now, six months later, my life is messy again!! It's all your fault!"

I'll break the news gently, dear reader: Being organized and clutter free requires practice and maintenance. No matter how good a book is or how great a system seems, if you don't keep it up, it ain't gonna work!

Lee Silber says it best in his book, *Organizing from the Right Side of the Brain:* "It's not getting organized, it's staying organized!" Staying organized is like staying on a healthy diet, he explains: "It's a lifestyle you have to maintain for a lifetime. You may fall off the wagon, but don't throw in the towel."

In other words, this is a journey, not a final destination. The organizing train doesn't end in a town named "Completion" where you never, ever have to do anything again. You don't ascend to a neat nirvana filled with categorized bookshelves and perfectly labeled storage bins. Just like being a great athlete or musician, being organized requires continuous practice. Otherwise it simply won't last.

Clutter will rear its ugly head if you don't continually reduce, purge, sort, and toss. Leftovers will host wild mold parties in your fridge if you don't clear them out. File cabinets, in-boxes, junk drawers, and closets will defiantly explode if you don't attend to their needs. Your calendar (and your life) will get overwhelmed if you don't practice the fundamentals you've learned from this book in an ongoing way.

The good news, says Silber "is that staying organized can be habit forming." So do a little every day. Remember to purge a few times a year. Keep reducing the amount of stuff you own. Make sorting, tossing, donating, and recycling part of your mindset. Prioritize your to-do list daily and review your goals at least twice a year because, just like the weather, people change. Remember that the point of organization is to support your life goals and create more comfort and ease in your everyday life. So adjust your organizational habits to support your life, not the other way around.

If you're still uncomfortable with organization, the truth is it may never feel like your most favorite thing. Cindy

Glovinsky, author of *Making Peace with Things in Your Life,* points out that organization "is like math. Some people are just better at it than others."

Even nuts-and-bolts time management expert Harold Taylor reminds us to take it easy. "The most important time management skill is to be able to recognize when you're overloaded. People are not generally time-deprived, but are simply trying to do too much." So make sure that part of your daily, weekly, and monthly maintenance routine includes time to do nothing in particular. Practice doing less, practice creating more space in your inner and outer world, and practice nourishing yourself—not just for a few days or weeks or months after you finish this book, but for the rest of your newly organized life.

It's time to create a "Keeping It Going Jar." Get a jar or a box (preferably one you'll enjoy looking at, as suggested in the "Contain" chapter). On separate index cards, list at least thirty-one activities you want to keep doing to stay organized. If they're large tasks, such as organizing the garage, break them down into smaller tasks that can be accomplished in ten, twenty, or thirty minutes. Put the index cards into the jar. At scheduled times throughout the week (choose how often feels right to you, whether it's once or five times), pick a card, set the timer, and take that small action. File desk papers for minutes; declutter your bulletin board; wash your kitchen floor; sort your in-box and action file; purge three files; declutter your medicine cabinet; review your master to-do list; and so on. When you've used up all the cards in the jar, give yourself a huge reward, and then dump them back in and start over again.

Collaborate

Remember that messy hall closet I mentioned in the introduction? The one with the stale water bottles and tap shoes? Originally, I tried to declutter and organize that closet myself. But the mere idea of organizing it overwhelmed me (let alone doing the actual work.) So I called up my good friend Patrice. "Work on my closet with me for a few hours," I begged. "Then I'll work on your office with you." She was thrilled. So we made a clutter-buddy date. She came over and we emptied everything out of the closet (just like the experts suggested), sorted it into boxes, repainted, and put everything back in ordered containers. Not only did the time fly, but we giggled and howled, took iced-tea breaks, and caught up on the latest books, movies, and gossip. Having a friend at my side was like magic. When it was finished, I felt like I could take on the most daunting of organizational challenges . . . as long as I had support!

Rejoice! The great news is that you absolutely don't have to do this alone. Life coach Natalie Gahrmann sums it up succinctly: "Support is helpful because we're human beings."

Don't think it's an imposition to ask someone for help. Years ago, I had a friend who always invited me over when she was cleaning out her closet. We were the same size and she had great taste. I'd help her organize her walk-in closet in exchange for getting first dibs on her fabulous wardrobe. As far as I was concerned, I went home the winner! So when you ask someone to support you in getting organized, you can offer them reciprocation, a meal, or whatever else feels like a fun trade for both of you.

Clutter-buddies can help you with everything from putting those shoeboxes of photographs into photo albums to shopping for the right storage containers. The advantage of friends is that your mess has no emotional charge for them. They can laugh with you or hold your hand when you burst into tears while tossing out those ancient love letters. They can offer fresh perspectives and ideas. And it's way more fun to have a garage sale with a friend (after you've both decluttered) than to do it on your own. Declutter coach Marilyn Nagel suggests using friends as part of your motivation and reward: Let's play tennis on Saturday or go to that movie if we get our kitchen pantries reorganized before then.

If you'd rather pay an expert to help, don't hesitate to hire an organizational coach. The money you invest will pay off, as long as they create systems that match your unique personality. (If you're right-brained, be sure to ask questions to assess their awareness of your style before hiring them.)

And don't forget what Dr. Charlene Belitz, author of *The Power of Flow,* says: Being in flow can synchronistically, and effortlessly bring the perfect support team to us-we just need to step out of the way.

In the end, remember what's truly important. Life is ultimately about relating, not achieving. When you're old and gray, will you look back over your life wishing you had decluttered the garage to ultimate perfection? Or will you wish that you had shown people more love and kindness? Organization is only worth it when it enhances our lives and leaves us with more time and space to enjoy ourselves and our loved ones.

Ask for help. Seek it out. And when it shows up, accept it gracefully and with gratitude.

EXERCISE

Make a list of organizational projects you'd like help with. Make sure to include particularly difficult ones (you know, the ones that make you want to cry and reach for a gallon of ice cream!). Then make another list of the people you'd like help from. Choose friends who are fun to be with and who also might need help themselves. Pick one project and make the call. Ask your friend to be your clutter-buddy. Schedule dates in your calendar (for you and for them). Block out a solid amount of uninterrupted time, and don't forget the iced tea and cookies!

Forgive

Every time Claudia opened her closet and saw those $350 lizard skin cowboy boots, she felt awful. She had bought them years ago, wore them only twice, and still felt like she had thrown her hard-earned money away.

Whenever Richard overbooked his schedule and had to cancel on someone, he got frustrated and angry with himself. With everything he'd learned about time management, he should know better. Yet he still, on occasion, screwed up some appointments, and ended up feeling like a loser.

Mistakes are part of being human. No matter how good our systems and our intentions, organization is an imperfect science. We forget to write something down. We skip our filing date for too many months, we overbuy and regret the cluttered results. Rather than beating yourself up about these inevitable missteps, remember to add one last step to your maintenance routine: Forgive yourself for your own messy mistakes and clutter-filled transgressions. And, while you're at it, cultivate an attitude of forgiveness toward other mess-making folks, too.

Jennifer Louden, author of *The Woman's Comfort Book,* insists, "No change is possible unless we accept where we are in the moment. Constantly raising the bar and demanding more keeps us stuck. So forgiveness simply acknowledges what is, without a story that it should be different."

If you find it tough to forgive yourself, one thing you can do is promise yourself that you'll try to learn from your mistakes. For instance, if you find that you have a tendency during the holidays to go on frivolous buying sprees, set a limit for the next year and allow yourself to stick to it. Consider the idea that traveling or celebrating a holiday doesn't have to necessitate buying a bagful of souvenirs. Enjoying the experience can be enough. Of course, getting organized is a process of changing habits over time. So if you do over-indulge, the most important thing to remember is to forgive yourself. Being kind to yourself and others will pave the pathway of successful organization.

EXERCISE

Throw away one mistake a day. Pick an item you wish you'd never bought and put it in the donation bin. Or forgive yourself for that missed appointment by saying a few words out loud, with intention and compassion, "I forgive myself and I release this mistake."

Celebrate

It was party time at Helen's newly organized townhome. She invited a group of close friends over to see what she had done and took them on a tour of every room in the house. For the first time in her life, she was showing off her closets! She even brought out "before" photos of the nightmares they once were. Everyone oohed and ahhed and Helen grinned from ear to ear. With dramatic flair, she flung open doors to all the cabinets under her kitchen and bathroom sinks. "Look at these!" she declared joyfully. "Don't they look great?!" Everyone applauded. And everyone told her how impressed they were. Not only did Helen feel great having a neater home, but she felt even better acknowledging and honoring the progress she had made.

Consultant Michelle Passoff recommends actually taking photos of your progress so you can see with your own eyes how far you've come. She reminds us, "The focus of organizing and decluttering isn't being neat and tidy. It's having a healthy, self-expressed life that communicates with others, and is in tune with the universe."

Honoring the distance you've covered on your organization journey, no matter how small, helps create that healthy, self-expressed life. One of the wonderful consequences of acknowledging our successes along the way is that in addition to making us feel good, it inspires us to keep going. Taking time to celebrate and enjoy what we've accomplished is a powerful motivator because it supports and amplifies our commitment.

As Jennifer Louden points out, "By not acknowledging our success, we cheat ourselves out of self-love. We perpetuate the idea that we're never enough out of fear that we'll become inflated and never do anything again toward creating the life we want. The exact opposite is true. Acknowledging and celebrating frees new energy to continue."

In the end, celebrating our progress is just plain old fun. And fun is one of the best motivators of all. (Don't forget to keep a sense of humor about all this, as well. Laughing, compassionately, at our own messy life, is a powerful tool to keep us going.) Staying organized is a lifelong journey. Applauding our progress, honoring the small steps we've taken, and enjoying that journey is ultimately what it's all about.

Break out the champagne (or bubbly apple cider) and throw an "I'm organized" party! (Don't forget to invite your clutter-buddies as guests of honor.) Pick a date. Invite friends and family over to witness your new order. Throw open your closet doors, show off your neatly arranged pantry, and offer up your new filing system and day planner for applause. (You don't have to give a grand tour of your whole house—just show off whatever you feel good about) Then share your newest goals with your friends. Let them be witnesses for your continued success. Announce the date of the next party, six months from now, when your backyard will be relandscaped and spruced up and your basement will be reorganized. Take the time to applaud your efforts, and provide others with the opportunity to celebrate and enjoy your achievements.

Experts Resource List

Don Aslett, dejunking guru, and the author of twenty-eight books, including *Clutter's Last Stand, Not for Packrats Only, No Time to Clean,* and *Clutter Free! Finally & Forever*
www.donaslett.com, www.cleanreport.com

Dr. Charlene Belitz, author of *The Power of Flow: Practical Ways to Transform Your Life with Meaningful Coincidence*
www.flowpower.com

Natalie Gahrmann, life coach and author of *Succeeding as a Super Busy Parent: 75 Practical Tips for Life, Love, Kids, & Career*
www.superbusyparent.com

Cindy Glovinsky, psychotherapist and author of *Making Peace with the Things in Your Life: Why Your Papers, Books, Clothes, and Other Possessions Keep Overwhelming You and What to Do About It*

Barry Izsak, president of the board of the National Association of Professional Organizers (NAPO) and author of *Organize Your Garage in No Time*
www.arrangingitall.com, www.napo.net

Jennifer Louden, life coach and author of *The Woman's Comfort Book: A Self-Nurturing Guide for Restoring Balance in Your Life* and *Comfort Secrets for Busy Women: Finding Your Way When Your Life Is Overflowing*
www.jenniferlouden.com, www.comfortqueen.com

Marilyn Nagel, declutter coach, professional organizer, and life success coach
www.marilynnagel.com

Michelle Passoff, international clutter consultant and author of *Lighten Up! Free Yourself from Clutter*
www.freefromclutter.com

June Saruwatari, Creator of The Organizing Maniac™ and cohost of TLC's *Home Made Simple*
www.organizingmaniac.com

Lee Silber, speaker, coach, and author of *Organizing from the Right Side of the Brain: A Creative Approach to Getting Organized*
www.creativelee.com

Karen Simon, owner of PC Tech Associates, a computer consulting firm for small businesses and individuals
www.yourpctech.com

Harold Taylor, time management consultant and author of fifteen books, including *Making Time Work for You*
www.taylorintime.com